The Only Survival Guide Teen Girls Will Ever Need

Understand Your Body, Learn to Take Care of Yourself, Establish Healthy Relationships, Make Money, Boost Your Confidence, and So Much More!

Aubrey Lee

3

advice. The content within this book has been derived from various sources. Please consult a licensed professional before attempting any techniques outlined in this book.

By reading this document, the reader agrees that under no circumstances is the author responsible for any losses, direct or indirect, that are incurred as a result of the use of the information contained within this document, including, but not limited to, errors, omissions, or inaccuracies.

Contents

FREE BONUS
SCAN THE QR CODE TO GET OUR NEXT BOOK FOR FREE

Introduction

Growing up, my mother never really understood how to approach the topic of puberty.

Take, for instance, the day I started my first period. I had heard a few things from my older cousins, but I wasn't completely sure; I went to my mother and sheepishly, hesitantly confessed that I thought I had gotten my period. Her response?

"Are you nuts? There's no way your period came. You probably have an infection."

She took me to the doctor, and as it turned out, I was right—but that wasn't the end of it. When I was 15, a teacher gently told me I needed to start wearing bras, to which my mother insisted the teacher had no idea what she was talking about; when I expressed an interest in shaving, she scolded me and insisted I should never shave, rather than teaching me how.

It was a difficult time for both of us. I am the oldest of three daughters, and while I was struggling to understand my body, my mother was in denial that I was growing up at all. I had to rely on my cousins for a great many things, and they were hardly experts; navigating my teen years was quite the ordeal. I often felt scared and confused. It seemed like nobody in my family understood me, let alone had any idea how to help me. The blind were leading the blind, so to speak.

My mother improved a lot with my sisters, giving them much better advice than she gave me, and I've also done my best to help them along their journeys. I'm very relieved to know they have the resources and support that I lacked, but to this day I still wish I'd had someone or something to teach me more: a person, a resource... or a book, like this one.

If you're anything like me, then you're uncertain and worried about your future as a woman. Growing up is one of the hardest things I've ever done. Puberty, social life, school, and beyond can all be unbelievably scary, especially when you don't have the resources or support you need to understand and navigate it. It feels scary to be isolated from people who can hold your hand through it, but this book aims to fill that spot.

Girls of all ages and experiences have shared their worries and woes with me, which I have collected and put in one place. This book seeks to address the concerns of young ladies just like you, aiming to answer all of your burning questions so that you can be equipped with the knowledge you need to make it through these next difficult years of your life.

Whether you are freshly 12 or an 18-year-old on the cusp of adulthood, there will be plenty of advice within these pages to assist you on your journey. Because it covers such a wide range of topics, you might already know some of the information we'll be covering ahead, or find some chapters more interesting than others. That's perfectly okay! You can use the information to help teach other girls who need that guidance, such as friends or siblings. Mentoring other girls through this period of transformation can form powerful bonds.

This book will explain the confusing mess that is puberty, teach you how to best take care of yourself, and aid you in self-discovery. It will teach you how to build a strong and supportive network, navigate social situations on and off the internet, and survive both your school years and those beyond. As it takes the role of friend and mentor, guiding you through this new journey, this book will show you that you are not alone: Your family is the best support a teen girl can ask for.

1

My Body Is Changing

"Hi, my name is Tonia. I am just 11 years old, and I'm getting very hairy all over, especially on my legs and armpits. Every time I look in the mirror, I feel bad. Adults say it's 'just puberty,' but I don't really know what that means. I don't know what to do."

When it comes to growing up, one thing is truly unavoidable: puberty.

It's the dreaded monster in the night, lurking behind every corner, forcing your body to grow in strange new ways and overloading you with new experiences that you aren't quite sure how to handle. Puberty can be a frightening experience for young girls, and it's a scary word to hear when you don't know what it means—only that it brings an abundance of difficult changes to your life.

Have no fear! We're going to go over *exactly* what puberty is, from the basic definition to all the ways in which it can change your body. Once we're done, you'll be prepared to face any and all of these changes head-on!

What Is Puberty?

Puberty is, in simple terms, the transition from childhood to adulthood. Beginning as early as 8 years old and as late as 13, it is a fluctuation of hormones and growth that marks your journey toward becoming an adult. It is a necessary part of life: Puberty allows us to mature so that one day we can have children.

While there is some overlap—primarily the growth of hair and development of acne—puberty is very different between boys and girls. You and your brothers or male friends will be experiencing different transitional phases, and this may make you feel isolated, but don't be afraid. When you know what to expect, puberty isn't all that scary!

How Will My Body Change?

Many of the hallmarks of puberty are physical—after all, the point of puberty is to push the body toward sexual maturity, so that humans can go on to reproduce and have children. There are a great many years between now and then, though, and plenty of preparations to be made in the meantime. Here are things you can expect to experience as puberty changes you.

Growth

Have your parents ever marked your height in a doorway? Perhaps you've noticed you're growing very fast, or even not at all. Maybe people remark on it, exclaiming that you're getting so big, or even that you're going to grow taller than them!

From the day we are born, we start to grow, but during puberty is when we experience the most dramatic change.

You will rapidly grow taller, and you will likely find that some parts of your body begin to grow out of sync with the rest. This is okay! It is especially common in hands or feet. You may need some time to adjust, and if you find that you're a bit clumsy because of it, don't worry. The rest of your body will catch up eventually.

You may experience a long period of growth or several small bursts; most girls reach their final height by the age of 14, or around the time of their first menstrual period. Any increase in height beyond this time will be minor—no more than 2 or 3 inches.

As you grow, you'll notice yourself begin to gain weight. Most of this will be around your breasts and hips, as they begin to develop in preparation for childbearing. Size and shape are determined by your genetics; if you've seen your mother's body, it can be a helpful indicator of what you can expect. This will usually begin with a "breast bud," which develops just under the skin of the nipple; with time, these will develop into full breasts. It is entirely normal for breasts to grow slowly, suddenly, or unevenly; they will sort themselves out with time.

Now, growth spurts can *hurt,* especially in the legs and breasts. You might experience a persistent ache, cramps, or stabbing pain. This is uncomfortable but normal. Using compression wear, wearing well-fitting, supportive bras, and applying heating pads can help alleviate pain. Stay strong, and remember that it is temporary! Once your body has reached physical maturity, you can say goodbye to growing pains.

Hair

You are going to grow hair. So. Much. Hair.

As mammals, humans have hair all over our bodies—the only place we lack them is our palms and the soles of our feet. When we grow older, that hair grows thicker and darker. Most of this will be on our legs, armpits, and genital region; as time goes on, it will become darker, and might even grow curly.

Body hair is completely normal! Everyone has it, even if they try to hide it. Don't feel bad if yours is darker or thicker than someone else's—it's all down to genetics and is nothing to be ashamed of. Some of us grow a lot more hair than others.

Body hair serves several key purposes in maintaining your health—allowing you to sweat, moderating your body temperature, and preventing nasty bacteria from reaching sensitive places. So, even if it's embarrassing, understand that your body is doing what it does best: taking care of you!

Menstrual Cycle

More commonly known as your period, menstruation may well be one of the scariest sounding parts of puberty. What *isn't* frightening about finding out you'll be bleeding for the rest of your life?

Well, a lot, actually! It's really not so scary once it's boiled down to the fundamentals.

You can expect your period to start about 2 years after you begin to experience puberty as a whole. A *period* usually refers to the 5–7-day period of bleeding, but the entire menstrual cycle is a month-long ordeal. Every month, your ovaries will release an egg into your uterus; this is referred to as *ovulation,* and it is an essential part of the reproductive cycle. After the egg is released, your uterus will begin to build up blood and tissue to protect it. If you do not become pregnant in that time, the egg and blood are then shed, resulting in the bloody ordeal we call a period.

The blood is not coming from an injury, so it does not hurt. It is only a tedious mess, which can be remedied with pads or tampons. It may look like an awful lot of blood or barely any at all; either way, you're only going to shed a few tablespoons at most each month, and it won't cause you any harm to lose it. Most people start

17

their periods light, and they grow heavier over time—mine was so light, I wasn't sure it was a period at all! Everyone will have a different experience.

However, you may still experience pain during this time; the uterus has to put in a lot of work to expel all that blood, and this can cause cramping and bloating. The same hormones responsible for cramps can also result in nausea, constipation or diarrhea, and even headaches. These symptoms usually arrive shortly before bleeding, and can persist for the entire period; this is called premenstrual syndrome, or PMS.

These symptoms can be reduced with exercise and a healthy diet, but the use of heating pads, hot baths, and even over-the-counter medications can help as well. If you choose to take painkillers or other medicine, make sure to follow the instructions carefully, and ask a trusted adult if you're not certain about the dosage.

Outside of your period, you may experience other vaginal discharge; it can vary from clear to a creamy color, depending on the point your body is at in your menstrual cycle. This is also entirely normal! Your vagina is self-cleaning; discharge can leave annoying stains on your underwear, but it is harmless to your health.

Skin

Acne. We all hate it. It's red and bumpy, and it can be itchy or painful. When I was young, I had downright *horrible* hormonal acne all along my jaw and a ton on my back.

Still, it's a normal part of puberty, no matter how annoying it is. Puberty affects the hormones controlling your skin glands just as it does everything else; acne is the result when those glands produce too much oil. The most common spots for developing acne are places that have the most of these glands. This includes your face, neck, back, shoulders, chest, and upper arms, but you can end up with a pimple or two anywhere. Be it whiteheads or blackheads, you're bound to have *some,* and some people's acne will be worse than others.

It may be tempting to pop those pimples, but even if it grants relief in the moment, do your very best not to! Popping pimples can make them hurt worse, result in unpleasant scarring, and even lead to the formation of more pimples. In the worst of cases, the site of a nasty pop could become infected and unpleasant. If you absolutely cannot help yourself, make sure to thoroughly disinfect the area, and use cotton swabs instead of your fingers, as you can minimize the spread of bacteria that way.

Always remember that acne will go away on its own, and if it doesn't, there are still less harmful options to get rid of them. Over-the-counter acne treatments using salicylic acid or benzoyl peroxide are quite effective in treating acne. If those are not enough, you should see an expert dermatologist; don't try to do their job for them!

What Mental Changes Can I Expect?

While much (if not most) of puberty boils down to physical changes, the hormones your body begins to produce and the fluctuations they experience can lead to extreme changes to your mental and emotional state. Fluctuations in mental health and even sexual curiosity are to be expected; all of this is natural, and with the right tools, you can navigate them safely and healthily.

Mental Health

As hormones change and shift, you can, unfortunately, expect to struggle mentally and emotionally. This is because many of the hormones that you will be producing differently—particularly estrogen, which increased drastically in women—are directly responsible for managing *other* hormones related to your happiness and stability. You may experience unexpected mood swings, anxiety, brain fog, and even depression. The biggest culprit of these is your menstrual cycle, which can cause particularly noteworthy mood shifts just before your period; PMS causes not only physical symptoms but also emotional ones. Add on the toll of physical discomfort, and you may find that you are especially easy to upset around the time of your period.

Unfortunately, hormones will not be the only culprit. As you and the people around you are going through puberty, social factors will become apparent; you may be exposed to ideas surrounding body image, social expectations, or even bullying. Since your hormones are so unpredictable at this time, these things can hurt you even more than normal. You may struggle with feelings of self-image, self-worth, and self-acceptance.

These factors can make everything difficult: maintaining relationships, focusing on your studies, taking care of yourself, and even waking up in the morning. It is a remarkably difficult struggle—one that millions of people go through every day. Understand that you aren't alone in this and that these mood swings aren't your fault. If you begin to experience these struggles, speak to a trusted adult for advice, be it a parent, caregiver, teacher, or counselor; if it worsens too much, consider asking for a therapist. It is never shameful to get help.

Q&A

How do I know when I should start wearing a bra? What kind of bra should I wear? What size? I feel so lost with all of the options. *–Alba*

For most people, it's simple: You should begin wearing bras when your breasts begin showing through your clothes, especially if they start causing any discomfort. The *breast bud* stage mentioned above is a good indicator that it's time.

When you first start wearing bras, you can usually get away with sports or training bras, which have simple small/medium/large sizing; padding is not usually necessary until you experience more development. As you develop more, many bra retailers can measure your chest appropriately, allowing you to find some that are comfortable and supportive.

Take care that you always wear a well-fitting bra; you can restrict your breathing and damage your ribs or lungs if they are too tight. Bras that are too loose, on the other hand, will provide no support and can increase back pain.

I'm getting really hairy. It's dark on my belly and thighs, and even a little on my breasts and chest. Is something wrong? Why is there so much? I feel like I look like a man. –*Liliana*

Hair can grow darker all over your body thanks to puberty. Not only can this happen on your stomach, thighs, and chest, but you could even end up with thicker facial hair! While this is understandably embarrassing, it is a normal phenomenon—some ethnicities are even known to have more body hair than others. This is due to higher levels of a hormone known as testosterone.

However, if this experience is not shared by your family members, or it is accompanied by other unpleasant symptoms, it could be indicative of an underlying hormonal condition. It may be worth seeing your doctor. They can prescribe hormonal treatment that will ease your symptoms and leave you feeling more comfortable.

I'm 14 and don't have my period yet. Is this normal? –*Christy*

Of course! Your period typically starts 2 years after puberty begins. For some people, this could be as early as 10; for others, as late as 15. If you're a particularly late bloomer, there's no reason for concern.

If it takes too long for your period to arrive, you may want to seek the opinion of a medical professional; there might be another reason you are not developing as quickly as expected.

I think I had my first period, but I'm not sure if it was or not. There was barely any blood, the blood was kind of brown, and it was only for a day and a half. I'm really confused. −*Marisol*

Periods can take many shapes and forms. It's quite normal for your first few to be very light, and the color of the blood will often vary. A darker brown color typically just means the blood is a bit old. Your period will likely fluctuate throughout your life depending on your overall health, including diet, exercise, and even stress; once you've had a few, you can determine what is or isn't normal for you.

Can I get pregnant if I've never had my period? − *Ariana*

Yes. While exceptionally rare, you will ovulate at least once before your first period, and this means you can get pregnant right beforehand. You can also become pregnant even if you're having your period so long as the egg hasn't shed yet, so always, *always* practice safe sex.

Is it okay for a 13-year-old to use a tampon? Am I still a virgin if I do? –*Shauna*

It is okay and normal to use any period products that you are comfortable with! Pads are the easiest for most people, but tampons are a good choice for athletics, swimming, or even particularly heavy bleeding. There are other choices, too—period panties or diva cups—so don't be afraid to experiment a little, and choose what is most comfortable for you.

The only thing that determines virginity is whether or not you've had sex. Until then, you are still a virgin.

My cramps are really, really bad, and I bleed a lot. Is this really normal? –*Ellie*

Cramps can be very severe, and bleeding can be heavy or light. However, if your pain is not resolved with over-the-counter medication or you are bleeding through menstrual products at an alarming rate, you need to see a doctor. This can be an indicator of an underlying health issue. Please tell a trusted adult and see a professional.

So, to Recap:

- Puberty is the body's way of transitioning to adulthood and reaching physical and sexual maturity.

- Puberty comes with many physical and mental changes, including hair and body growth, the start of the menstrual cycle, and a difference in mental health.

- The changes that come from puberty are completely normal, and nothing to be worried or ashamed about.

Now that you know what to expect from puberty, we can move on to our next topic: How to take care of yourself in the midst of all of these changes.

2

A Crash Course in Self-Care

"Hi, I'm Jenny. I shower and wash myself well, but I'm still getting lots of acne, and I stink ALL the time. I keep gaining weight, too, and it's making me feel really down. I feel like I'm doing something wrong. What could it be?"

I remember how hard it was to maintain my body when I first started puberty. Even though just a bath was

27

enough to keep me clean before, now I was starting to stink just a couple of hours into the day—not to mention I was sweating buckets. I was eating the same amount of junk food, but it was suddenly starting to make me gain weight. Those nasty zits started popping up on my face, and every time I got rid of one, it seemed like another 10 would replace them! It was *so* annoying, and it really wore down on my mental health, too.

There's so much going on in your life at the time you start puberty, and it only gets busier from there. It's easy to miss out on the skills you need to take care of yourself, and it can be embarrassing to ask others for help when you feel like you should already know what to do. Luckily, this chapter is all about self-care— everything you need to know about maintaining both your physical and mental well-being is right ahead!

Physical Health

The biggest, most obvious changes that occur throughout puberty are physical, and they're the most often talked about pain points among teens. It is frustrating to deal with all these new physical changes, especially when you're really not fond of the transformation. Gaining weight, smelling bad, and sweating all the time is not an enjoyable experience, after all—but there are steps you can take to make life a lot easier, and feel much less gross!

Hygiene

Hygiene is essential not only for your health but also for your comfort and happiness. At your age, you probably have at least an idea of the basics—showering, brushing your teeth, and washing your hands.

If you haven't gotten into a regular hygiene routine yet, now is the time to start! While many children can get away with infrequent bathing, once you reach puberty, you're fighting more than dirt and mess to keep yourself clean and presentable. You're going to find that you sweat more, your feet and armpits stink, and your hair and face produce a lot of oil. You'll probably find that you need to shower at least once a day, paying special attention to those difficult areas.

Soap and shampoo are not one-size-fits-all. While some people can get away with using just about anything, pay attention to what your body is telling you. You may have dry or oily skin. You may have a dry scalp or dandruff. Take note of these things, and look for products that can address your problems.

Keeping your face and hair clean will help in the management of acne, but be kind to your face and use gentle products; hot water and scrubbing can dry out your skin, which can *increase* acne. As I've mentioned before, products containing salicylic acid or benzoyl peroxide can aid immensely in the management of acne; try starting first with products meant for sensitive skin, until you have a gauge for how much your skin can handle.

It's important to know that while showering appropriately will remove body odors, the fact of the matter is that it usually doesn't last. Body odor is caused not by sweat itself, but by bacteria on your skin that produces a smell when you sweat. As such, you're going to want to start using an antiperspirant deodorant. While these words are often used interchangeably and most deodorants are also antiperspirants, it's important to make sure you're getting something that does both— antiperspirants keep you from sweating, while deodorants have a nice smell to cover anything underneath.

Bear in mind that antiperspirants will not do the job of a shower! At the end of the day, you still need to scrub off all that gunk.

Vaginal Health

At least once, you've probably worried if your vagina stinks—everyone does, and it's a source of a lot of embarrassment for girls.

The thing is, *every* vagina has its own smell. *All* genitals do, including a man's penis. It's nothing to be ashamed of. Your objective shouldn't be to eliminate the smell; the simple act of wearing clothes and taking good care of yourself is enough to make sure it doesn't become an odor that bothers you or other people.

While standard hygiene is usually enough to make sure your vagina is doing fine, it's still important to know the dos and don'ts:

- **Don't** use perfumed or scented soaps. These can disrupt the pH balance of your vagina, which will cause discomfort and ultimately make any odors worse.

- **Do** use warm water. You can use mild, unscented bar soap if you really feel like you need to, but water will be enough in most cases.

- **Don't** use a loofah, sponge, or washcloth. These collect all sorts of bacteria, which can lead to bacterial vaginosis.

- **Do** use your hands. Make sure they are clean, including under the fingernails.

- **Don't** clean inside your vagina, where it enters your body. This part of your vagina is self-cleaning; you're more likely to dry it out by cleaning it, which will cause discomfort.

- **Do** clean the outside, the *vulva*; this includes the "lips," or *labia,* and the skin around them. Just like any other part of your body, you want to make sure it's not collecting sweat and bacteria, as well as blood from your menstrual cycle.

Keeping your vagina happy and healthy is essential to your comfort, as well as keeping that odor in check. Take note of any discomfort, and keep an eye on any discharge to make sure it is a healthy clear, white, or gray color. Abnormalities don't always mean something is wrong, and even if there is something wrong, vaginal conditions are rarely serious if caught early; still, you should take any and all concerns about your health to a trusted adult, or even a doctor.

Period Maintenance

When it comes to your menstrual cycle, naturally the question follows: How does this change my hygiene habits?

That breaches a topic we've only touched briefly on before: menstrual products. Pads, tampons, cups, period panties... so many options, with their own pros and cons. How are you supposed to choose?

The biggest two factors to consider are your comfort and blood flow. That said, you can consider the following when choosing your menstrual products.

Pads are usually the most accessible to girls who are first starting their periods, as they come in all shapes, sizes, and absorbency levels, so you can experiment to find one that works for you. They stick to your underwear and absorb blood as it sheds from the vagina. Most are disposable, but reusable pads are another option. Despite their widespread use, some girls find them uncomfortable because they dislike the moist feeling, or they liken the padding to wearing a diaper.

Tampons are another popular choice. They're inserted into the vagina using a cardboard or plastic applicator, and they absorb the blood before it exits the vagina. It can take some time to get used to them, but many girls prefer this option because of its versatility; athletes find it easier to perform physical activity, and it is a great option for going swimming during your period. Still, tampons are not for everyone; some girls find them uncomfortable no matter the application or absorbency level, and others still need to supplement their tampons with a pad or liner to prevent spotting from leaks.

Menstrual cups, much like tampons, are inserted into the vagina to collect blood before it can exit. They're made of silicone, which makes them reusable, and unlike tampons, they create a seal in the vagina to prevent blood from escaping. They can also be worn for up to 12 hours! Some women find them difficult to use, however, and removal can be quite messy, as they collect the blood rather than absorb it. **Menstrual discs** perform a similar function, but they are disposable, and rest higher up in the vaginal canal than a cup.

Period-proof underwear, or period panties, are a form of underwear meant to absorb menstrual blood much like a pad or tampon. They consist of several layers that both absorb blood and keep the moisture off of your skin—so, unlike pads, they do not feel wet all day long. They are washable and reusable, and if you take good care of them, they can last up to 2 years. Still, many girls find that they prefer only to wear period panties on days of light flow, just in case; ladies with heavier flows may use them to supplement a tampon, rather than trusting the period panties alone.

Your options may feel a bit overwhelming at first, but you have decades to figure out what works best for you. Take as much time as you need!

Appearance

One of the greatest concerns for the average teen girl will always be how she looks. It's hard to be a teenage girl. This is around the time that everyone—from your family to your classmates to even random strangers—starts to expect you to put work into your appearance. It's easy to *say* not to worry about what others think, and another to put it into practice. Our main goal is to foster confidence and make you feel good!

Grooming

Shave? Don't shave? It's a rather hotly debated question, isn't it? Most importantly, *how?*

The best time to start shaving is when *you* want to. Ask yourself—is this for an aesthetic reason or a practical one? Are you shaving your legs to make them pretty, or because you like the smooth feeling? Your armpits because it's nicer to look at, or to ease up on the sweating? Your pubic region because you hear that other girls do it, or because it makes your period less messy?

Every reason is valid, but you're better off doing things for yourself than for others.

When it comes to shaving, no two girls do the same thing, but there are a few tips to get you started:

- **Shave in the same direction your hair grows.** You can adjust this as needed, as some women don't have such sensitive skin, but it's the best way to avoid razor burn.

- **Change your razor frequently.** They dull very quickly, and a dull razor is more likely to cut you or give you razor burn.

- **Soften and hydrate appropriately.** A hot bath and a hydrating soap or gel will make the skin harder to cut and the hair easier to get rid of.

- **Consider electric trimmers.** They don't shave as closely, but they're often good enough, and just a tad safer to use.

- **Be cautious of hair-removal products.** They work magic, but they're also a common skin irritant and even an allergen. They also have no business being around your vagina.

Makeup and Fashion

As much as any book wants to be the authority on modern looks, the fact of the matter is, times are always changing, and nobody can keep up with every trend. My mother, for example, fell victim to a trend of ultrathin eyebrows, and now she's got them for life!

Rather than looking at current trends (which often only suit a rare few people anyway, and often end up wasting money when a new trend pops up), consider what you can do to shape your own look and style.

Makeup is an expensive hobby. To many, it is not just a way to make themselves look pretty—it is an art form. Not everyone will be good at it, nor will everyone enjoy how they look with makeup on. It's entirely your preference. With this in mind, consider how badly you want to get into makeup, how often you want to do it, and how much time you have to put it on before your daily obligations, and go from there.

Start small with foundation and a bit of eyeliner, and consider adding products as you go along. Many makeup stores offer services where you can have your makeup done by an expert, and they're also more than happy to explain the use of various products. Just be careful they don't overwhelm you with sales pitches!

Whatever you decide on, remember that makeup is not very kind to your skin. You'll need to keep up a very thorough skincare regimen if you want to wear makeup daily.

Fashion will never be one-size-fits-all, and in a world of fast fashion, designer brands, and stick-thin models, it can often feel inaccessible. The best way to persist through it all is to develop your own style.

Draw inspiration from models who look like you, and take note of the sorts of things they wear and why they're flattering. Different body types—not just weight and height, but their shape, such as a pear versus an apple—will look good in different clothing. Consider the sorts of things you gravitate to on your own. Do you like hats, bracelets, or scarves? Is there a particular pair of shoes you're attached to? Try to build outfits around those.

Above all, use trial and error. You have plenty of time to develop a style that looks good and feels like you!

Mental Wellness

With so much discussion around appearance and wellness, it's easy to forget the strain it can have on your psyche—as well as other stressful factors in your life, which, as a teen, feels like *everything*. It's absolutely essential to remember to take care of your brain as well as your body.

Rest and Relaxation

When things start to feel like too much, the most valuable thing you can do is *relax*. Step away from the things that are stressing you out, and pursue things that calm you down and help decompress. Consider the following options:

- **Going outside.** This may seem like a no-brainer, but in the 21st century, it's easy to get wrapped up in staying indoors, hovering over a book, or staring at a screen. Vitamin D deficiency can lead to fatigue and even depression; sitting on the porch and soaking in some sunshine can genuinely affect your mood.

- **Partaking in a hobby.** It's easy to forget the things we love when faced with more important issues that need to be addressed first. Set time aside to read, write, sing, dance—anything that brings you joy. You don't always have to be productive!

- **Trying meditation.** While not for everyone, people who *do* enjoy meditation benefit greatly from the introspection and relaxation it brings. There are a thousand resources for guided meditation—you can look online, or even at your local library.

- **Socializing.** Teen life is so busy, and most socialization is done through schoolwork or at home. Get outside and meet your friends somewhere, even if it's only a park. You could even just lie in bed and video-call them. No school, no obligations—just good company and good times.

- **Taking a hot soak.** Hot baths are great for physical relaxation, which contributes to mental relaxation. Consider using bubble formula or Epsom salts, lighting a candle, and playing your favorite music. Settle into the atmosphere and let it ease away your worries.

Self-Improvement vs. Self-Acceptance

With all this talk of making yourself better, it can be easy to lose sight of the real goal: *feeling* better.

Remember that the goal is not some idealized form of a teen girl, but the happiest, healthiest form of *you*. You don't have to be perfect, and you don't owe anything to anyone. While it's important to take care of yourself, remember that even if you don't do everything right— even if you don't eat all your vegetables, go on hour-long runs every day, or consistently shave your legs—you are still someone worth love and support.

Accepting yourself as you are is the first step to improving. Be kind to yourself, every step of the way.

Q&A

I wear pads, and blood gets *everywhere*. It cakes and gets all sticky when I can't get to the bathroom right away. What can I do? –*Maizie*

This is actually the exact reason I started to shave before my period! I found it made cleanup a lot easier. Of course, not everyone wants to do that—and on that note, don't shave during your period. Your skin is too sensitive at that time.

You might consider carrying feminine wipes around with you to help with cleanup, whether you're home or at school. There are tons of options out there; much like cleaning your vulva normally, look for unscented wipes for sensitive skin. We don't want any irritation.

My discharge is slightly brown. What does this mean? Am I sick? *–Jan*

Brown discharge usually means there's a bit of blood mixed in—it might replace a real period, or it might come just after your period. There's no concern here!

Discharge is a concern if it's yellow, green, thick, or cheesy, or smells particularly bad. Vaginal itching is also a telltale sign something is wrong. *Always* see a professional when you have concerns about your vaginal health, because most issues don't go away on their own.

What is toxic shock syndrome? Should I be worried about it? *–Kaitlyn*

Toxic shock syndrome (TSS) is an extremely rare condition in which bacteria gets trapped in the body and makes you severely sick. While it's often associated with girls wearing tampons, the reality is that anything that

43

hangs out in your vagina for extended periods of time can cause TSS—including contraception.

Realistically, most women will never experience TSS, but I completely understand if you want to avoid tampons just to be certain. If you still want to use them, you'll be much safer so long as you stick with lower-absorbency tampons and make sure to take them out on time.

If you ever do end up with TSS, *do not wear tampons again*. It's very common to get TSS again after the first time, which we do not want.

Does underwear matter? I'm worried mine will be called granny panties, or childish. And what's the deal with thongs? –*Demi*

The cut of your underwear! Go with what is comfortable and makes you look good. If someone's going to make fun of your panties, they're not someone you want seeing them anyway.

When it comes to material, you want to stick with cotton. Lace or silk may be cute, but they don't let your vagina get any air, which can result in uncomfortable dampness and even infections.

44

Thongs aren't recommended, ever. They encourage the spread of harmful bacteria to your vagina. Skip the string; wear something with more coverage.

How the heck do I find a makeup look that works for me? There are so many styles and options! *–Millie*

Your best bet is honestly to look online! There are hundreds of beauty gurus on the internet, all with different faces and styles. Consider the shape of your face and each of the features on it: For example, eyeliner on monolid eyes will not be the same as eyeliner on hooded eyes. The thickness of your lips and the shape of your cupid's bow can impact your lipstick style. The undertones of your skin determine what colors suit you best. Look around, play around, and see what you like!

I really want to amp up my wardrobe, but clothes are so EXPENSIVE. My mom only lets me buy one thing at a time. How am I supposed to work on my style like this? *–Claudia*

Ah, the limits of a parent's wallet. We've all been there. My advice? Thrift, thrift, thrift!

Sure, thrift stores are full of a lot of nothing, but you can find some real treasures on those hangers. Just for a few dollars, too! Be it a top you just can't live without or designer boots (can you believe I found a pair of Louboutins at a thrift shop for 20 bucks?!), it's worth the visit, and you get a lot more bang for your buck.

It's also seriously worth looking into upcycling! See an oversized patterned button-up that would make a killer dress? Find some patterns, make some cuts, sew a seam or two, and now you've got a stylish new piece *and* a useful new skill under your belt!

So, to Recap:

- Make sure to maintain good hygiene every day, no matter what.

- Vaginal health is incredibly important to maintain, so make sure to take good care of your vagina and use appropriate products.

- Do your best to maintain a healthy diet and exercise well.

- When it comes to your looks, develop your own sense of style instead of following trends that might not suit you.

- Above all, remember to be kind to yourself, and take a step back if you're getting overwhelmed!

With all of the tools in your pocket to take care of yourself, it's time to move on to the next question: Who *is* the girl you're taking care of?

3

Getting to Know Myself

"My name is Adriana, and I'll get to the point: I don't really know who I am. I feel like everyone already knows what they like, who they like, and what to do with their lives... meanwhile, I just eat, sleep, go to school, and watch TV. How can I be more unique and interesting?"

Ah, identity. For most of your teen years, the act of growing up is guided or even taken care of without your input. You're told how to succeed in school, your body

49

grows all on its own, and your parents enforce responsibility and routines you'll be following for the rest of your life. The thing you have the most control over is who you are as a person, and determining that can be an intimidating task. Here, I hope to help you figure out exactly who it is you are, who you want to be, and how you can get there!

Remove Obstacles

You are in control of yourself, but there are still obstacles in this world and within *you* that can prevent you from taking those reins. Forming your identity is a difficult matter, after all—it may even be scary. It's easy to fall into doubt or passivity and to simply allow life to happen without giving yourself any real input.

Silence That Inner Critic

I remember standing before the mirror several times throughout my teen years and thinking, *I am unbelievably boring.* My journals were filled with pages upon pages of self-doubt that couldn't be quelled. My hobbies felt boring. My looks were too dull. I wasn't funny or cool, and I faded into the background of friend groups.

Who is it that decides whether you are unique, interesting, cool, or not? Believe it or not, it starts with *you*.

We *all* worry that we aren't good enough—that there is something inherently wrong with the way we look or act, and that people won't like us. We are often the first to point out our flaws, and if we don't believe ourselves to be interesting, how can we expect anyone else to?

Stop. Take a step back. Imagine someone you love thinking this about themselves. Imagine yourself saying this to someone you love. Does that feel okay? Does it feel *right?* Certainly not.

It can be frightening to drop self-criticism—I, myself, worried that there might be nothing left without it—but you cannot grow when you are actively stifling yourself. Be kind and patient. You are still only a human, and you deserve compassion and patience, even from yourself.

Speak for Yourself

With so much of your life governed for you by your family and school, it can be hard to find your voice. When conflict begins to arise between what you want and what you are *told* you want, it may be frightening to contradict these people, and you may opt to stay quiet to keep the peace.

Don't let anyone stifle you. You have a voice—use it. Parents may have good intentions, but the reality is, it's hard to keep up with the wants and needs of an entire other person, and what they know about you can quickly become outdated. Don't be afraid to tell people what it is you actually want.

It may be even more difficult when they are *right*. Some people keep on top of things and know you extraordinarily well. What's the harm in letting them speak if they're taking care of you? Still, you cannot rely on them forever. Someday, you're going to have to navigate the world without people to speak for you. You need to learn how to handle yourself before that day comes.

Passivity has no place when it comes to defining yourself. Take charge now, so you can be secure in your identity throughout your life.

Ask Yourself...

Nobody can decide for you who you are, but there's an upside to that: You're the expert! There's a good chance you already know more than you realize. You just need to know where to look. There are dozens of questions you could ask yourself—these are just meant to provide a good place to start.

What Am I Good At?

Look at your hobbies. Do you enjoy outdoor, sporty activities? Do you like arts and crafts? Does technology interest you? If you aren't sure about your hobbies yet, the best thing you can do is simply try them! Attend beginner classes, join clubs or teams, and look up tutorials online.

If you're not so sure about hobbies, you can also glance at your school grades. Are there subjects where you consistently score highly, or classes you always look forward to? Perhaps your teachers have even taken an interest in the work you turn in, or left praise on your schoolwork. They're likely to have opportunities you can pursue further, such as advanced courses.

Be it academic or extracurricular, there are fruitful career paths for just about every interest in the world, and with practice comes perfection—so, don't shy away from the things you're good at.

What Do I Like?

This question isn't limited to skills or abilities—what do you *like?* What are some of your favorite things?

The things you enjoy and surround yourself with can provide insight into who you are as a person. Your

54

favorite colors, animals, and even foods can say a lot. For example, you might find someone who likes orange or yellow to be sunny and friendly, or someone who prefers cats over dogs to be quieter and more reserved than their peers. Your taste in music can often reveal the inner workings of your thought processes or emotional state.

Pause and ask yourself, what do your favorite things say about *you?*

How Do Others See Me?

To be clear, this is not a question of opinion, but of *description*. Think of your parents. If asked about you, they might describe you in comparison or contrast to your siblings. They might say you're louder or quieter, or more or less social, or remark on your level of responsibility. Your teachers, on the other hand, would likely talk about your work ethic. They'd point to how well you listen in class, how efficiently you work with others, and how quickly you understand the source material. Your friends might speak of the way you interact with others. Would they consider you loud or calm? Outgoing or reserved? Are you more of a leader or a follower?

You don't have to fill in these questions yourself, necessarily. Most people have no problem answering the question of how they see you. Don't be afraid to ask around, and pay attention to any reoccurring answers—though we can present differently to everyone, there's a grain of truth in every perception.

Who Do I Want To Be?

Do you know who you want to be when you're older? It's such a popular question, and sometimes it feels like everyone knows the answer. If you don't, that's okay! Plenty of people struggle to respond. Knowing yourself now is one thing, and seeing the path you want to take in the future is another.

This is where we look elsewhere to find inspiration. My mother once told me that every person in your life leaves a piece of themselves with you, and you carry that piece forever. In this way, the people we love and admire become a part of us, just as much as we define ourselves.

Who do you look up to? This could be friends, parents, teachers, or even celebrities. Why do you look up to them? Is it their personality and the way they treat others? Is it the kind of work they do, or the success they've found in their careers? You might be inspired to start a band after reading the success story of your favorite singer, or motivated to volunteer for charities because a friend you love does the same.

You should never copy someone's entire self, but seeing the good in others is a driving force to create good in *you,* and it's a great path for finding yourself along the way.

Seek Meaning

What motivates you to be yourself, and what does being yourself motivate you to do? For some people the answer is simple—it's for themselves. Happiness, comfort, and self-satisfaction.

Others may need a bit more help, and there's nothing wrong with that. Some of us need to set goals beyond identity or need a bit more guidance on what to do with ourselves.

Personal Power

The most important part of being yourself is taking charge of the matter, and finding power over that which you discover. Stand firm in your identity. Don't allow yourself to be swayed, and don't settle for unreasonable or unfair criticisms. Know your worth, know your strength, and know yourself.

Knowing your worth directly translates to knowing what you *deserve,* as well. The things you seek today, as well as the future you strive for—be it success, love, happiness, or whatever else—you must find the confidence to reach for it. Once you have it, you must maintain the knowledge that you worked for it, and thus you deserve to have it.

Keep in line with who you are, strengthen your resolve, and you will become a powerful person who succeeds in whatever you put your mind to.

Finding Spirituality

Religion is a tough topic to crack open. Everyone has had their own brushes with it. You may already follow a religion, or you may not know where to start. Religion is not for everyone, but though it often goes hand in hand with *spirituality,* they are not the same thing.

You may already practice spirituality if you are religious; prayer is the most common form. You can also seek opportunities to study your religious texts, meditate on your teachings, or serve your community. Religious leaders can offer guidance not only in matters of your faith, but also in how to handle other aspects of your life in relation to it, and how to define yourself under that banner.

Even without religion, there are opportunities to deepen your sense of self and understand your meaning in the grand scheme of things. Many nonreligious spiritualists turn to our relationship with nature, or where we stand in the wide expanse of the universe. Meditating on these topics, journaling about them, and even taking spiritual trips to further your understanding of the topic can help define your sense of self among it all.

Choosing to Be Good

When developing ourselves and deciding on who we are, the most important part is to become someone *good*. This can range from general kindness and surrounding yourself with good people, to making an effort to do good for others and improve the world around you. What is the purpose of identity if it is not something we can be proud of?

You don't have to make grand efforts. Excessive positivity can be a detriment to your own mental health, and you shouldn't forget yourself in the service of others. You are allowed to make yourself a priority—but still remember to treat others well, and show kindness whenever the opportunity arises.

Q&A

I'm super interested in woodworking, but the materials are really expensive and my parents are worried it's too dangerous. How can I convince them? *–Annabelle*

Well, for starters, I do think that's a fair concern to have. You're their daughter, after all, and while you're certainly capable of being careful, accidents still happen. Additionally, we have to be realistic—money *is* a limiting factor in most people's lives.

That said, if there are ever any hobbies that interest you but have a high barrier of entry, look around for workshops in your area. They provide safe environments with the appropriate tools already available, where experts can teach you their craft and oversee your safety.

You might show up and decide the work isn't for you, in which case, no harm done. On the other hand, you could go and find that you're even more set on the idea! If you continue to attend them and make good progress, it will be a *lot* easier to convince your parents that it's a good investment in your future.

I keep trying, I really do, but I just can't bring myself to believe in my family's religion. So much of it feels contradictory, or I just really

strongly disagree with the messages. I feel stifled. *–Zoe*

Believe me, I'm not a stranger to this topic. Growing up, I had hyper-religious family members who turned me off the idea altogether. I even wondered if it had any real value—some things about it just seemed so needlessly cruel.

The wisdom has come to me with time that it isn't up to us to debate the value religion has to others. We really can't know for sure, in the end, who is right—and studies even suggest that religious faith is good for mental health!

Whether or not you choose to follow a God, spirituality can still enhance your life greatly. I've found my own peace through it, and if you have any interest in it, I encourage you to seek out the stories of millions of others who have made their own spiritual journeys.

But if you just don't believe in it, that's really okay. It isn't for everyone. While it provides a lot of comfort and a sense of security to many, you don't need to believe in some higher power or grand design to be a good person or have a strong sense of self. How you feel and what you want triumphs over what other people want for you—but remember not to be needlessly critical of those who *do* believe.

I don't know… what if people don't like me, or who I am? What if I never settle? What if I'm like this forever? –*Peggy*

This is something a lot of people struggle with. I definitely did when I was younger. Between schoolwork and basic self-care, I felt like I just didn't have the time to really develop, and for a long time, I didn't even try. I didn't feel like I had the skills or traits necessary to thrive as a person, and I lived feeling that way for a long, *long* time.

It's really easy to preface this answer by saying, "Don't care about what others think! Focus on your own perception." But I feel like it's also relevant to point out that *things change.*

The thing is, we live for a long time. Eighty years is no joke. Every thought, feeling, and opinion we have—they very rarely withstand the test of time. As people, we're not capable of remaining stagnant; we always grow and change. If you're not satisfied with who you are today, show yourself some patience and kindness. You have your entire life ahead of you to find the person you want to be.

Growth is inevitable, so long as you keep your heart and mind open to it. Sometimes, some of us just need a bit more time than others.

So, to Recap:

- Your teen years are a time for self-discovery and defining who you are.

- In the pursuit of your identity, consider the things you and the people around you already know, and expand on those ideas.

- You are the authority on this matter, so don't allow obstacles on the path to finding yourself.

- There is a great power in knowing yourself, and putting it to good use for yourself and others.

Finding yourself is only one part of the battle—next, we'll discuss how to take this new girl and help her build relationships!

4

Surviving Social Relationships

"Hi, I'm Hannah. Is it usually this hard to make friends? Friends, and then there are boyfriends, and I barely even get along with my siblings. More than making friends, how do I keep them?"

Honestly? To some degree, yes—it is that hard.

People are incredibly diverse. There is no way to please everyone, nor can you appeal to every single one of them, and as such you cannot hope to get along with every person you meet. Some people will love you, some people won't be able to stand you, and most people will fall somewhere in the neutral middle—and the feeling will likely be mutual!

When it comes to each sort of relationship you'll encounter down the road, there are three key factors to keep in mind: forming the relationship, maintaining the relationship, and when you should consider ending it.

Developing Friendships

Many would argue that friendships are the most important bonds you can form over your lifetime, and I'm inclined to agree. Out of the people who have had the most impact on my life as a whole, the vast majority of them have been close friends. Whether they're made only for a day or two at an event, or you keep them in your life for decades, friends can bring an unmatched light to your life that you'll remember forever.

Making Friends

The very first thing you have to do when making a friend is introduce yourself! This is often the hardest part of making friends. One of the most unfortunate habits of people, be it teens or adults, is to fear an honest greeting. We love to stand around and do nothing, waiting for someone else to make the first move—but you have to get out there and say it! Sit at that lunch table, walk next to someone on your way to class, strike up a conversation with the person next to you. Give a hello, give them your name, and ask for theirs. You'll get plenty of practice over the years, and I guarantee you most of those people will be happy you had the courage to take that first step.

The next task is to maintain that momentum. Starting a conversation can be difficult—you have to find a topic, and keep it up for long enough to seem interesting without forcing it. This is a skill you'll hone over time, but for now, you can stick to common topics any teen can relate to: schoolwork, weekend activities, or even their hobbies or out-of-school commitments. The easiest topics are ones that ask people to talk about themselves, and they're a good way to immediately gauge what sort of person they are—and if you have anything in common!

If you're struggling for a good way to close the conversation, the best way to do so is to end it concisely, instead of standing around trying to get a final interesting word in. Try doing so by asking for their contact information. It's a universal sign that you need to go, but you want to talk again; if they give it back, the feeling is likely mutual!

Congratulations! You just survived your first conversation with a new acquaintance. Now what?

Maintaining Friends

Some people find the initial connection easy, while deepening the relationship eludes them. After all, it's easy to use the word "friend" in reference to someone you know, but making sure you connect enough to actually *be* friends is another story.

The best way to maintain a friendship is truly to just keep talking. Use that contact information you got before, and don't be afraid to strike up conversation again over text (I would suggest holding back on a call until you've discussed schedules and how you both feel about calling, as it makes a lot of teens nervous). If you're still not sure what to say, follow up on a conversation from before! Discuss a class they said they liked, or ask about an interest they mentioned in passing. It will make them feel heard, and they'll open up more to you.

If you have common interests, this is a great way to really dig into a friendship. You can plan get-togethers or outings around those interests. Alternatively, you could try introducing each other to things you like. If you have something in common that you're both interested in but haven't tried yet, try doing it together! Forming a new common interest is a great way to strengthen a bond.

As time goes on, you'll find it easier and easier to just hang out without any real plans or guidance. Congratulations! That's a friend!

In Pursuit of Love

Ah, love. Heralded as the be-all and end-all to relationships, the final goal in teen movies, the ultimate objective in life. While it's true that love is a wonderful part of life, it's also something that teens like to rush into with reckless abandon, leading to a whole lot of heartbreak. Every relationship in your life will be filled with trial and error, but romantic relationships definitely see the brunt of it—you're looking for a singular person who will make you happy and stay in your corner for the foreseeable future, after all, and that can be a seriously tall order for anyone to fill.

Be patient, and pursue relationships with an open mind and consideration for others.

Finding That Someone

Looking for friends can be a very wide, generalized search. There are acquaintances, friends, besties, and even fair-weather friends, all of whom have their time and place. When it comes to partners, though, we have a tendency to be a *lot* more choosy, and reasonably so! In that case, it's quite understandable that you shouldn't go trying to find partners wherever you can, and you probably don't want to.

That's usually where crushes come in. Maybe it's just someone cute you saw in the hallway, in which case you can use a lot of the same tips and tricks as when developing friendships, or it could be that you're developing affection for someone you already call a friend. If they're already your friend, that could make it a lot easier, or a lot harder—your foot is already in the door to knowing them well, but you may worry about ruining your friendship for the sake of something that might not work out. Either way, you may be nervous, but there's a key piece of advice in situations like this: You'll regret more that you missed an opportunity than you will that you took an opportunity!

Consider light compliments, like calling them cute or praising a skill they have, to put across that you have romantic interest. Invite them out, but don't dance around the topic. Make it clear that you're interested in dating them, because it's going to be really awkward if you're not on the same page.

Be patient, and be mindful of your expectations. You're both still young, after all, and the future is still a long way away; don't expect the other person to be ready to sign up for a long-term commitment, and you shouldn't jump right into that, either. Knee-jerk crushes can be

71

fun at first, but quickly fall apart when you realize they're all looks and nothing else that you're looking for; take your time, and get to know each other better before you jump into a relationship.

If things go well, then go for it! If they haven't made the first move but you're confident that the interest is mutual, don't wait around forever. Ask them out! Even if it's scary, take the leap. As the saying goes, you miss every shot you don't take.

Keeping That Someone

So—you've got a partner. Congratulations! It's something to be happy about, and you're more than entitled to be. But once that honeymoon phase is over, you're onto the next part: maintaining the relationship you worked so hard to land. It's easy to get lost in the high of even having a relationship, but once you come down from that, you have to consider what it is you *both* want out of this.

You know what you like about this person—do you know what they like about you? What do you know about each other? You should always make an effort to learn more; people can surprise you with information that you'd never know unless you went seeking it out. What is it you both want out of life? How do you see your future panning out? How do you fit into one another's lives? These are all questions worth asking, and you really don't want your answers to clash.

While you want to have a few things in common with a partner, there will inevitably be places where you don't see eye to eye. Having a difference of opinion is normal; sometimes, those clashes may be more extreme. So long as they are not extreme ideological differences, these can still be overcome. If you really like this person, make an effort to resolve it together! Listen patiently and with an open mind, express yourself clearly, and try to come to an understanding. Accept your differences as they are, and grow together past the conversation. You want to be supportive to your partner, and vice versa—a healthy relationship is one in which they are in your corner, even if they don't necessarily agree with you.

Closeness is important in a relationship, of course, but don't forget your friends in the process. Try not to monopolize one another's time. You both have social needs outside of each other, and obligations to attend to that romance can easily interrupt. Try scheduling certain times that are just for you and your partner, and focus on other things otherwise. As much as you might want to spend every waking hour with your partner, it's just not healthy to ignore everything else, and clinginess may even drive one or both of you to grow tired of one another. Besides, absence makes the heart grow fonder!

When to End Things

As much as we might want our various interpersonal relationships to be forever, and may even promise these things to one another, the fact of the matter is that you're still young, and nothing is guaranteed to be permanent. Sometimes, we need to step back and cut our losses; as I said before, you can't hope to befriend everyone. Some people are better off as acquaintances, and some people shouldn't be around you at all.

Consider the following reasons for a friendship or relationship to come to an end, and determine if the ties you've formed are ones you'd be better off without.

Natural Reasons

It doesn't have to be something dramatic. Maybe you think they're kind of boring, and you don't look forward to hanging out. Maybe you just don't have that much in common. Maybe they have different priorities when it comes to their relationships versus other obligations. Maybe you don't feel that initial spark anymore, and don't feel like you love them. Maybe this is all the case, but in reverse, and you don't feel like they're as interested in you as you are in them.

This sort of thing happens. Sometimes, people just don't "click." You don't need to force it; gently distance yourself from this person. There doesn't have to be any bitterness involved. There are people out there who you will *both* have a better connection with, so it'll benefit you both to move on.

Red Flags

As preferable as it is to let things go for easy, peaceful reasons, sometimes you have to step back and realize that a relationship is actively unhealthy.

Do you struggle to be yourself around them, or feel like they're hiding things from you? Do you feel like you fight over the smallest things? Do they pressure you to do things you don't really want to do, regardless of their nature? Does your partner lie to you, or cheat on you? Maybe you find their overall behavior distasteful, even uncomfortable; even if they aren't mean to you directly, they might treat their other peers with disrespect.

A really good indicator that this friendship or relationship is bad for you is if the other people in your life don't like them. Do they fight with your friends? Do you hesitate to introduce them to your parents? Other people can usually see the bad things that you may be blinded to because you care; it can be scary to take a step back and realize you've been ignoring red flags, or you may even feel lost when you think about the time you've wasted on someone who doesn't care about you the same way you care about them.

It's a really tough situation, but there is support for you. It is always best to rip the bandage off quickly; don't spend any more of your time or energy on someone who makes you feel bad. There will always be someone better.

Extreme Circumstances

It's one thing for someone to be generally kind of nasty and mean spirited, and another altogether for them to be dangerous.

Verbal abuse is covered somewhat by the previous section, and it is undeniably a serious situation; verbal abuse negatively impacts your self-image and often makes you feel trapped. It could be that this person makes cruel comments about your appearance or behaviors, either to you or to other people. Maybe they yell at you over the smallest things. Perhaps they threaten extreme behavior when you do something wrong or consider breaking things off with them. It is common that these people cut you off from your friends and family, and make you feel as though they are the only person who could ever tolerate you.

Physical abuse is usually quite a bit more obvious, but you may wonder how people can simply allow themselves to get caught up in a physically abusive relationship. It may start small and become worse with time; when paired with verbal abuse, you may start to feel as though you deserve it somehow, or it isn't that big of a deal. This is not true. People should never seek to harm each other physically, and if anyone in your life ever tries to hurt you out of malice, you should *never* tolerate it. There are some situations in which forgiveness is dangerous to your safety, and this is one of them.

Peer pressure is another huge factor in this. If the people around you often engage in unsafe behaviors, such as underage drinking or smoking, abusing street drugs, or partaking in illicit activities such as stealing or tagging, you should consider just how good friends they really are. It can be one thing if they only do it themselves; it is another if they try to pressure you into it under the guise of being cool or grown-up. Even if you do not personally partake, these sorts of people are often unhealthy and can bring other dangers to your life. Do not put yourself in harm's way by befriending them. "Street cred" is not worth the danger, and even if you survive the ordeal, you risk ruining your future opportunities in life.

None of these are tolerable behaviors. You should avoid people like this at all costs; if you've already become close to them, you need to cut all contact immediately. Still, this can be frightening; dangerous, cruel people can become aggressive and make serious threats when it comes to breaking off relationships. Please don't be afraid to reach out to a trusted adult for help in this matter, no matter how hard these people may have tried to cut you off from your friends and family. They will ensure your safety, and call in the proper authorities if need be.

Q&A

What if I don't want friends? I'm okay alone. – *Alexis*

I understand where you're coming from. I was a very isolated, quiet kid, and I didn't feel like I needed or wanted any friends for a very long time. And you know what? That's *okay*. Maybe you like your peace and quiet, or being alone, or what have you. Maybe conversation is hard, or you're just anxious about the ins and outs of maintaining those relationships. We really can't force ourselves to make friends—it's not genuine, and it's unfair to the other person.

But something I learned later on is that friendships are *crazy* important to making our lives easier down the line. If you don't have friends, you'll struggle to navigate all sorts of other social aspects of life: pursuing career opportunities, taking care of financial obligations, or even ordering your food in a drive-thru! These are things I still struggle with today because social relationships are just that important to our brain development.

So, even if you don't make *friends,* try to at least keep a good passing relationship with your classmates. Acquaintances are fine. Just make sure you are fulfilling at least a little bit of that social quota, and you'll thank yourself down the line.

And who knows—maybe you'll make a friend in the process!

Where do I FIND friends? Can I really just pick anyone? –*Bridget*

Yes, you really can!

Still, if you're nervous about talking to random kids in your general education classes or people on the same bus as you—which I totally understand, because it could be awkward if things go wrong—look at the other things you do in your spare time!

Are there kids your age at your church you could befriend? Are you in a club or on a sports team, or do you take specific extracurriculars? These are great candidates for potential friendship, because you will already have something in common with that person. It's a great place to start, and an easy way to strike up conversation!

If you find you're too nervous to make friends in person, or you just really don't have many opportunities, you can consider online spaces as a start. However, you want to be *very* careful when navigating the web, which is luckily a topic you can look to the next chapter for advice on!

There's a girl I don't want to be friends with anymore, but she's not taking the hint and I don't know how to cut it off. What should I do? – *Taylor*

This is a really tough situation to be in. It can feel cruel to decide that you don't want to be friends anymore, especially if that person seems to like you. Still, you don't owe anyone your friendship, no matter the situation—stand your ground on this matter, no matter what you do.

The best thing you can do in *any* situation like this, whether it's a friendship or a romantic relationship, is be honest and open about it. Whether you have this conversation in person or over the phone is your choice; some may claim that doing these things over text is the coward's way out, but I think that's unfair. Sure, there are better ways to handle things, but if you're not comfortable in a relationship, you shouldn't be obligated to follow a specific set of social rules to get out. That's one of the easiest ways to end up trapped in a situation that makes you unhappy.

Be gentle, but concise; explain that you're glad you got to meet her, but you don't want to be friends anymore. Make it clear if you don't want to talk anymore. It may just be that she didn't understand the cues you were sending; give her a chance to be let down gently.

As much as I want to say it's that easy, it is possible she won't take this well. If she continues to text and call, block her contact wherever necessary; if she harasses you in person, please don't rise to the bait. Instead, take it to a trusted adult. They can talk to her about her behavior, and if she doesn't ease up, they can make an effort to reduce the amount you see each other, so you can continue to have a peaceful time.

So, to Recap:

- An essential part of growing up is forming relationships with others.

- The biggest keys to forming long-lasting relationships are a strong, confident start, and maintaining them with attention and care.

- Not every relationship is meant to last; know when to step away, both for your own sake and the other party's.

- Avoid dangerous situations, and don't be afraid to reach out to others for help.

With these tools in your pocket, you have everything you need to start making friends and seeking love in your day-to-day life. The real world isn't the only place our social life extends, though—in the next chapter, we'll discuss how to navigate things when the internet is involved.

5

Safety on and off the Web

"My name's Penny, I'm 16, and I struggle to keep friends in real life because I have really niche interests. When I do make them, we usually chat over messenger apps instead of meeting face to face. Why don't I just make friends online? It seems a lot easier and more convenient that way."

We have to admit that in this day and age, if you aren't a

part of the digital world, you're left behind.

Now, I'm the last person to discourage you from exploring online spaces. I grew up with a home computer, and I've made dozens of online friends, many of whom I've stayed friends with for years. It would be hypocritical of me to expect you not to meet people and interact with them online. However, the internet has gotten more complicated since my first days on it—and, with that, more dangerous.

It used to be that people were overly cautious on the internet; now people aren't cautious enough. We're going to remedy that here, and talk about how you can keep yourself safe on the internet.

Before You Start

To begin with, there are a few things you should be aware of when it comes to using the internet. Why you're using social media and what you can expect to encounter are important things to straighten out.

Pros vs. Cons

Social media certainly has its ups and downs. Some see it as a technological marvel and an irreplaceable part of today's society, while others lament the impact it has had on people and the connections we make with one another. Many aspects of social media are a double-edged sword, providing both benefits and harm.

Information about the goings-on of the world is easier to access through social media. Topics you otherwise might not have heard about can find their way to you through the screen, and it makes social advocacy very accessible to passionate youths. However, this can also negatively impact mental health; social media sites have a tendency to constantly flood with bad news, which can result in exhaustion and negative worldviews.

Socializing over the internet can have both positive and negative impacts on teens. If there is something that prevents you from making friends in person, be it a disability, anxiety, or a lack of opportunity, the internet can make it much easier to come out of your shell and introduce yourself to others. However, social media trends can also push you to act unlike yourself, and too much social media can negatively impact your ability to interact appropriately with others. The potential anonymity of online spaces can also encourage the prevalence of bullying; without any means of identification, it is easier for some people to be cruel and hurtful.

Learning can be greatly aided online, with infinite

access to educational resources and the ability to talk to friends and classmates who can help. Files and videos can be shared freely to everyone's benefit. However, social media undeniably also provides a great hindrance to education, as it's far too easy to become distracted by your phone or computer and lose track of time.

Before you go about creating your social media profiles and making friends, consider these things in full, and be cautious not to become absorbed in your screen time.

Be Safe

Whatever is said about the dangers of the internet, the reality is that you're probably going to use it anyway. In this day and age, social media is becoming a necessity, be it for personal use, school, or even your future job. With that in mind, there are some key ways to keep yourself and your information safe.

Information Security

When it comes to navigating online spaces, the worst thing you can do is provide public access to your personal information. With it, people you do not know could find you in real life, steal your identity, commit crimes under your name, or even hurt you personally.

There are certain things you should *never* post online. These include:

- addresses

- phone numbers

- birth dates

- Social Security numbers

- legal identification

- financial information

Never, *ever* post this information publicly, do not share it through messages unless it is an emergency, and ensure that any website asking for it is fully trusted. If you are not sure, *always* ask a trusted adult to verify, and err on the side of caution.

Anonymity

The easiest way to keep yourself safe online is to remain anonymous. While the vast majority of the people you meet online are just like you—a normal person with no ill intent—it only takes one bad apple to make things dangerous for you. If people do not know who you are, they cannot do anything harmful with the information.

With that in mind, consider the following steps to protect your identity:

- **Do not use your real name.** While it is common to use usernames, ensure that you are not using any part of your name for it. Though it is generally safe to use a first name with people you've grown to trust, I still must encourage you to avoid it; if you want something more personal to use with online friends, consider nicknames based on your favorite things.

- **Avoid sharing your location.** Do not tell people the names of your schools, workplaces, churches, or anything else that could identify your location, and censor any images that display the relevant information, such as local storefronts or street signs. It is generally okay to share what country or time zone you reside in.

- **Be cautious with personal images.** Selfies may be a dime a dozen, but generally speaking, you don't want to share your face online with anyone you don't know. Be careful with pictures of your bedroom, pets, or home, and censor any identifying information—and don't show off your family, either!

In the case of websites that encourage a more personal touch, be thorough with your privacy settings. Consider making your entire account private, so that only people who are your friends can see your information, or limit the people who are allowed to follow you.

Curate Your Space

Unfortunately, it's very easy to find yourself in places online that you really don't want to be. All over the internet, you can find opinions that ruffle your feathers, information that upsets you, and unkind people who seek to upset you. Without realizing it, social media can go from a fun activity that broadens your horizons to a miserable experience that has you arguing with strangers all day.

Instead of wasting your time on something unpleasant, curate your space to one that you can enjoy.

Step One: Remove Negativity

Use the block button, and use it liberally! I remember that at first, I was frightened to block people; it was seen as the coward's way out, and I hated the idea of caving to something that upset me. That is just what unpleasant people want you to believe! You don't owe them your time, and you shouldn't waste it as such. It's also worth noting that anonymity isn't only for the sake of safety—privacy settings can also prevent people you just plain dislike from seeing anything about your life.

It's also worth noting that you can often mute topics that you find upsetting. If your social media is full of unpleasant news, trends, or other topics, look for functions that allow you to see less of them. Some websites are more adept at this than others.

Step Two: Invite Positivity

Seek out and follow things that interest you. Look into music, hobbies, entertainment, and even people you enjoy, and fill your social media feed with these things. Remember that most algorithms function based on interactivity; if you like something, make sure to interact positively with it! Like it, share it, and comment on it, and the website will notice that you enjoy it and show you more. In this way, you can ensure you always have nice things to look at online.

There are often spaces catered to people just like you, who enjoy the same things that you do! You can find these with minimal effort most of the time, and they're a great way to find like-minded people who won't cause you trouble. If there are a few bad apples, just remember step one—out of sight, out of mind!

Warning Signs

Of course, while there are plenty of preventative measures, sometimes things still slip through the cracks.

Scammers will lie and cheat their way through by trying to acquire your information. Be wary of anyone you don't know trying to ask you for anything. They may pose as an authority, a giveaway, or a friend of a friend. Usually, scams are easy to spot, because they're not particularly believable; even if something does sound like it could be true, do *not* trust it. Anyone who genuinely *needs* your sensitive information will go through official channels to request it. Above all, most scams can be poked through simply with a bit more thought—you likely haven't entered any giveaways, your friend has no idea who this person is, and the authorities would be contacting your guardians, not you!

Hackers can be quite scary. They take your personal information, and a great deal of crime can then be done with it, from selling it, to identity theft, to stealing from you. The good news is that as a minor, these things are very unlikely; additionally, they generally require you to have given sensitive information to someone you do not know. Hackers may try to obtain this through blackmail or extortion. Never offer your private information to anyone unknown, no matter what they threaten you with; the backlash from denying them will never be as bad as what will happen if you give them what they want.

Predators are the greatest risk to teens online. It is not impossible for adults and teenagers to share online spaces safely, but you should always be cautious of people much older than you. Keep the conversation with them public and within age-appropriate topics. Just like in real life, if any adult ever lures you into an uncomfortable or private conversation or asks for information they are not entitled to, inform a trusted adult, report their conduct to the appropriate online authority, and cut contact immediately.

Q&A

I have this really annoying aunt who I can't just block, or she might cause trouble. What do I do? —*Kendra*

Ah, this is a very tough problem to have. I went through something similar, but I'm pretty confrontational—at some point, my problematic family members were the ones to get tired of me and block me! But I don't really encourage going around and causing trouble like I did.

Instead, consider muting them! Most sites have a function for exactly this purpose: You can go to that person's profile, mute them, and you will still be "friends" without you having to see any of their posts. On some sites, you can also exclude specific people from seeing your posts. Overall, you'll be able to avoid interacting at all with that person.

If they're causing you a lot of grief, though, consider sitting down with your parents and talking it out. If this family member is really that troublesome, there's a good chance your parents will be in your corner. You can then block that person, and your parents can defend you if they start any drama over it.

One of my online friends keeps asking to meet up in person. Should I do it? How do I know if it's safe? –*Amelia*

I have successfully met several online friends in real life. Heck, some of my family's closest friends were ones they met online! But when it comes to meeting people you only know from the internet, there is *always* a risk.

First, ask yourself if this is a reasonable request. Are you two close friends already, or have they brought this up spontaneously? Do they ask often, persistently, or is this a rare opportunity for you? How well do you two actually know each other? Carefully consider whether this is the behavior of an excited friend, or someone eager to get you alone. If you're hesitating, there's probably a good reason, even if you aren't sure why. Listen to your gut.

Ask your friend for the contact information of a trusted adult in their life, and allow them to speak with your guardians. If your friend has good intentions, this should be no problem at all. They can discuss a safe meetup, in a public location with plenty of foot traffic. You should *always* bring at least one trusted adult with you to meet anyone from the internet. This is good practice even when you get older.

If your guardian puts their foot down, please, *please* listen to them. There is undoubtedly a good reason, and your safety comes first.

Is sexting okay? What about sending risky photos? *—Sadie*

Neither of them is a good idea, honestly. You must remember that you are a minor. You have to navigate anything concerning sex with great caution—not only for your personal safety but also for legal reasons.

When it comes to sexting with a same-aged partner, realistically, it's not going to land you in any real trouble. It may be embarrassing if it gets out, but ultimately it's not dangerous. However, you should *never* sext with anyone online, as you have no idea who they are or what they want from you.

Sexual photos, however, should *never* be exchanged, under any circumstances. All it takes is a bit of peer pressure or one bad breakup and your partner could send those pictures to anyone, and that's not even touching on how bad it could be if a stranger got ahold of them. As well, these photos are considered child pornography in most countries; being a teenager does not protect you from legal punishment if you're sending or receiving risky photos. Save it for when you're an adult.

So, to Recap:

- Social media has its own pros and cons, all of which you want to consider before diving in.

- Remember not to get too absorbed in social media. Other aspects of your life are more important.

- Always stay safe on the internet, and don't be afraid to ask for help if things get out of hand, just like in real life.

Having discussed the ins and outs of socializing both on and offline, we're shifting focus back to you, and what a growing girl wants for herself. Step one: Finances.

6

Money Is My Friend

"My name is Kayla, and I'm 16 years old. I'm trying to keep up with trends and friends, but I don't get an allowance—just whatever my mom is willing or able to fork up at the time. How do I make money? I don't want to keep freeloading, and I want to have my own disposable income."

Money is a tool, a resource, and an obstacle in life.

When I was a teenager, I fought tooth and nail to have

my own source of income. My family was just too poor to fork out allowances to one kid, let alone all of us, and it was extremely rare that we were allowed anything extra at the grocery store. I jumped from side gig to side gig, landing a proper job as soon as I was able, and never looked back.

There are a lot of things that factor into finding work and making money, but by far the best resource you have is determination!

Where to Work

As a teenager, you have somewhat of a different job market than adults. While there are plenty of careers you obviously can't take as an inexperienced kid, there are also jobs that are a *lot* easier to land when you're young. Consider the following options when searching for your next money-making venture.

Odd Jobs

Odd jobs are often the first place teens start when it comes to making money. These are things found around friends and family, or through word of mouth; mowing lawns, dog-walking, car-washing, babysitting, and cleaning houses are all popular choices, and can be quite lucrative for teenagers. These are jobs that professional adults can do, but it's often easier and cheaper to allow a teenager to do them—and some people just like to show a bit of compassion to a young person who wants some spending money.

Ask around friends and family if they need any of the aforementioned jobs done. Lawnmowing is an example of one that can be done by asking door to door (make sure a trusted adult is nearby when you're doing this). There are also odd, one-off jobs that people may have available; I've personally cleaned gutters, housesat while homeowners were on vacation, and helped meal prep with a mother for a week.

Work to Your Strengths

Even as a teen, if you're old enough to work, you've probably already settled on some strengths you've developed. You can turn these into money!

If you're an artist or graphic designer, commission work can be quite lucrative, be it advertising online or contacting local businesses. If you excel in a particular course at school or even an instrument, you can become a paid tutor. Writers can make a decent amount by submitting pieces to newspapers or charging for report writing. Do you garden? You can sell extra produce to neighbors, or at a farmer's market!

Consider what you're good at, and how you can monetize the things you already do every day.

Proper Jobs

Not to discredit other forms of revenue, but odds are, they just won't match up to a proper job at an established business.

As a teenager, most of your work opportunities will fall into food service or retail—really, there's nothing wrong with these. They have a low barrier of entry, and many places will take just about anyone while providing decent pay. But for me, at least, those things *really* weren't my cup of tea; there are other options! Libraries, senior homes, animal shelters, nurseries, and daycares are other popular picks for teenagers that might align more with the things you enjoy doing.

You can also look at summer gigs, such as being a lifeguard or camp counselor, or even ask around if you know any family or friends who own a business!

Job Preparation

If you're looking to get a proper job under a known company, it's going to take some extra work from your end. Sure, just about anyone can get hired for anything, but there are plenty of things you can do to make yourself into a more appealing candidate for the job!

Licensing and Certification

As much as you can just go out there with absolutely nothing under your belt and still get a job—you're only a teenager, after all, and you probably *don't* have any experience—there are workarounds to this!

Licenses and certifications are evidence that even if you haven't necessarily worked in a particular field, you have the relevant knowledge necessary. Some of these are quite niche, and may only apply to one or two jobs. However, licenses in particular computer programs, food handling, or even lifesaving can carry you a long way!

You can get certifications on just about anything, with most courses to obtain them being cheap and just needing an easy, one-time payment online. Some particularly common courses, such as CPR and food handling, may even have local programs that allow you to obtain them free on certain dates. Do your research, and if nothing else, your family will probably be more than willing to spend a little to help you prepare for the future.

Résumés

Résumés are an often feared beast when it comes to job hunting. There are plenty of excellent resources online that provide outlines for a good résumé, and there's a good chance you've had at least one opportunity at school to create one. As a teenager, you might think you don't have anything to put on a résumé, but this just isn't true! If you've done any odd jobs at all, these things still count.

As well, you can look at any time you were a part of a club, team, or volunteering activity—any time you went out of your way to participate in something special or extracurricular. If you are an honor student or have received any awards for your talents, you can also list these achievements.

Your experiences can provide a jumping-off point to list your strengths. Consider the sorts of responsibilities you had during these times; for something as simple as babysitting, you can list preparedness from the unpredictability of child-rearing, organizational skills as you planned meals and activities, and time management because you had to keep track of the child's personal schedule alongside your own!

Interviews

The very word is a little scary, isn't it? Never fear— getting to the interview stage is already a good sign!

Interviews come with a lot of preparation and posturing. You want to look and speak professionally, give and invite respect, and make yourself an extra attractive candidate to the hiring manager. Wear your Sunday best and arrive around 10 minutes early, and you'll be showing the interviewer already that you're eager to get started!

When it comes to preparing for the interview, you'll of course want to have some answers ready to questions about yourself, including your strengths and weaknesses; be sure not to go too hard on the latter, and consider listing things that may also be strengths, such as being *too* detail-oriented. Questions that sound scary to some people include ones about the company and why you're a good fit, but these are easier to answer than you realize! Look back at the job listing, take a look at the company's website, and write down the many ways you fit into each requirement and how you align with their ideals. Ask an experienced adult to help you with a mock interview to prepare you for the real thing!

After your interview, send a quick thank-you email. It doesn't have to be long or exceptional, but thanking them for their time and for considering you will make you stand out among other applicants. It can really be a deciding factor for the hiring manager!

If you don't land the job, that's okay! There are thousands of opportunities. Take a small break, get your courage back, and try, try again!

Other Considerations

Getting a job is all well and good, but once you have it and the money starts rolling in, there are other factors that come into play—primarily, responsibility with said money, and balancing this new part of your life with everything else you have going on.

Budgeting

Now, you may be thinking: I'm only a teenager. What do I have to budget? And honestly, you may not have anything yet. Maybe you're incredibly lucky, and all of your expenses are covered for you, work related or otherwise. It's still in your best interest to start saving now, while you lack other expenses. And, of course, the most important part: You're forming good habits for later down the line!

Budgets can be calculated with ease once you have a good grasp on how much you make per paycheck. As tempting as it is to spend all your new bucks on whatever you want, restraint is key! Consider how much you spend on wants versus needs; you can subtract money spent on necessities from your monthly earnings, and the new amount is what you will budget.

Whether you divide your income into dollar amounts or percentages—personally, I prefer the latter—you'll want to decide how much you allot to extra expenses versus savings, and stick with it! You don't have to cut out frivolous spending entirely (even as an adult, I'm prone to impulse purchases!) but you want to ensure you're doing so within reasonable bounds.

Your savings can provide a safety net in case of emergency, a starting amount toward a car or apartment, or can even help with college expenses!

Work—Life Balance

As good as jobs can be for teaching you responsibility and kick-starting your financial journey on the way to adulthood, sometimes it just isn't realistic to work as a teenager.

Maybe you have too many other obligations, and the extra workload is burning you out. Perhaps you don't have enough time for everything, and you find yourself regularly running late. You could struggle to prioritize, and your grades might start to fall behind. Maybe you're just plain-old stressed and feel you're not cut out for this.

No matter the reason, it's okay. Your priority as a teen should be your schooling; anything that gets in the way of that is something that gets in the way of your future. If you need to quit, there's no shame in it—just make sure you do so gracefully, with the appropriate 2 weeks' notice in writing.

Q&A

My parents don't want me to get a job. How can I convince them to let me work? —*Liz*

There are a dozen reasons your parents might not want you working. It may be that they're worried you can't

111

handle it; in this case, the best thing you can do is show how you can. Take up extra responsibilities around the house, maintain your grades, and try to have a genuine conversation (not an argument!) about their concerns and how you can soothe them.

However, it could just be that it's not realistic for the household. Maybe they need you at home, taking care of the house, or they can't afford to get you to and from interviews, let alone work. This, too, can be worked around—assure them that you can take care of both work and home responsibilities, and look for work close by home so you can walk there.

Above all, *talk* to your parents. You won't understand their perspective if you don't have a conversation. And when it comes down to the wire, if their position is firm, listen—they have their reasons, and they're usually good ones!

What if I'm no good at working? Will I be fired? Will it make it hard to get another job? *—Patty*

Honestly, there's a good chance you'll be fired from at least one job in your life—as my mom told me, best to get it out of the way early! Getting fired as a teenager really isn't that big of a deal.

Every job is different, and each of those jobs has its own idea of a "best fit." If you aren't cut out for the job, that's not necessarily a poor reflection on you. That's just how the cookie crumbles sometimes! Since you're young, it's not likely to be a financial strain, nor are employers going to raise a huge fuss over it.

Consider why you were fired, and how you can improve on the reasons listed. Take a small break from working if you need to recover—getting fired can be quite the emotional blow—and when you're ready, get right back to job hunting! If an interviewer asks about it, the best thing you can do is be honest and mature about the reason you were terminated; a future employer will appreciate the honesty, and you can take the opportunity to express a drive to grow and improve from the experience.

So, to Recap:

- When looking for a job, consider your options and what best suits your financial needs.

- Build a strong résumé and prepare thoroughly for interviews.

- Spend your money wisely, and start saving early!

- Know when it is time to let go of a job and prioritize yourself.

A job is just one aspect of growing up—next, we'll discuss your outlook after high school, and what the future holds for you!

7

My Life After High School

"I need help—my name's Lila, I'm graduating in a year and a half, and I have no idea what to do! Options for college, work, internships... it's all so much. I feel dizzy, and it's like everyone either knows exactly what their plans are or they're even more lost than I am. How can I pick a college? What if I don't want to go to college? What if they don't want me? What do I do?"

After 12 years of constant school attendance, it's pretty normal to look at the end of it and think, "What now?"

There is often an immense amount of pressure to go straight to college after completing mandatory schooling, but in reality, you have a wealth of options! College is the right choice for many people, but not everyone, so we'll go over several different opportunities to help decide which is right for you.

Schooling

The most obvious choice for fresh high-school graduates? More school. Not everyone is eager to dedicate even more of their lives to schooling, but for some career paths, it is necessary to continue to attend courses and learn. Even within this route, though, there are plenty of options.

College

The preferred pick for anyone pursuing a degree, college is a popular choice. Continuing your schooling for just a bit longer can really open up your access to certain life opportunities, and that's not even touching the opportunities you can find through simply *being* in college.

It can be confusing, however, to look at the endless list of learning institutions available to you and try to figure out what the best option is.

Colleges are divided into different types of institutions that provide different experiences and benefits. Consider your goals going forward; if you've already decided on a career path, you can consider colleges that specialize in that career field. If you aren't sure what you want to do, you can look at taking some time at a two-year college, such as a community or technical college, which will help you get certified, obtain an associate's degree, or acquire credits in general education while you are deciding on your future plans.

Whether you opt for private or public, two-year or four-year, college or university, it's going to take a lot of research to find the right one for you, so it's time to start looking! Important considerations include if you're willing to travel, what size campus you want to deal with, whether you want to live on or off campus, and how much money you have to play around with. With these things in mind, make yourself a list of your ideal schools and apply, apply, apply!

Trade School

Do you want to learn a new skill and get into a solid job, but college is too long, expensive, or otherwise unrealistic for you? Consider learning a trade!

Trades include special skill sets—usually in the fields of construction, technology, medicine, or manufacturing— that you wouldn't otherwise learn. These are usually hands-on jobs that are best learned through direct experience and apprenticeships; think building or repairing things. Your electrician, for example, is considered to be in a trade career.

Trade schools are often far cheaper than college, and they go by *much* faster. Skilled trades are in high demand for workers, as fewer and fewer young people are going into them; because of this, they pay better money than just about any other job you could land so soon out of high school. Accessible and lucrative, learning a trade is not only an easy alternative, but an intelligent one—even should you choose not to continue down that trade path, the skills you learn could be invaluable later in life!

Other Options

As we've already mentioned, schooling isn't everything. Whether you're simply not interested in a career that requires additional education or it isn't accessible to you, there are other options to pursue as you exit high school and begin your adult life.

Straight to Work

Sometimes, you just want to jump right into the workforce, and I'm here to tell you that's definitely an option! Some people spend their entire lives working at a retail or food service job. My mother *loves* her work as a waitress, and she's been doing it for decades! Even today, she easily supports herself and her husband on her income.

Jobs that are considered entry level like these are easy to land, and it's easy to move up the ladder. It is quite common to go from a normal clerk, to a supervisor, to a manager; so long as you work efficiently, your bosses will take note of your usefulness and be eager to put you to work elsewhere. As well, experience from entry-level work is easily transferred across playing fields into countless other jobs!

Military

In many places, the military is a viable alternative for high school graduates with few other options in life. While not an attractive option to everyone, it's especially common along low-income families. Serving one's country can be an honorable pursuit, and it comes with a wealth of benefits.

Not only do you get a base salary, but many military branches and programs include a sign-on bonus; additionally, you can look forward to affordable (if not free) health care, plenty of paid and family leave, and retirement and pension plans. As well, a popular reason to join the military is the aid they provide with tuition, debt, and loans. Not only will military benefits help you as an individual, but they can assist if you already have or are thinking of starting a family.

It's also worth a reminder that military jobs do not all see combat. They have as much use for paper-pushers as any other line of work. You can find a cozy, safe job in the military that comes with all of the benefits and none of the stress!

Helpful Programs

When it comes down to the wire, sometimes you're just lacking in resources across the board. Luckily for you, there are programs all over the world to help you make the transition into adulthood.

Perhaps most well-known, there are plenty of work assistance programs whose job is to get you hired wherever possible. They will help build your résumé, apply to countless places, and put in a good word, and some even provide additional financial aid so long as you prove you are making a real effort to get hired.

If you live with a disability, you may need additional help before you're ready to go into the workforce or pursue a higher education. Vocational rehabilitation programs are funded by the government, and they will evaluate your abilities and needs, help train you to work, and can even provide financial aid for schooling. If your disability is deemed too severe, you can also look into financial and housing assistance programs for the disabled.

Some programs are even available to offer a full-ride package to disabled or low-income youths, such as the U.S. Job Corps. So long as you fulfill the requirements, you can land yourself a spot with lodging, education, and job training all provided. These programs often last several years, and can even help struggling young single parents.

This is only the tip of the iceberg; it's worth contacting informational lines and government assistance organizations yourself to see what your options are.

Q&A

I haven't been able to decide on what to do with my life. The options are so overwhelming, and I feel like I'm running out of time. What can I do? *—Eva*

Have you considered taking a gap year?

This stress is common! I also felt crushed by the amount of options and decisions to be made. Take a step back, breathe, and try to look at the big picture. How urgent is it for you to go to school or work right away? There's often a hurry to pick right out of high school, but this isn't always necessary. If you can, consider taking some time off from it all so you can make a more informed decision.

If need be, you can still work a part-time job, or consider volunteer work so your résumé isn't empty during this time. A gap year is a good time to broaden your horizons, and help settle on and prepare financially for the future you want to pursue.

A gap year doesn't have to be a year, either—it could be a handful of months, or even longer than a year! So long as it is sustainable, it's okay to take your time.

The price of college is so steep in the United States. I don't know how I can ever hope to afford it. What are my options? _–Tori_

You have quite a few of those, actually!

Scholarships are my first suggestion, and though they can sound intimidating to land—not everyone is a straight-A honor student with academic or extracurricular awards under their belt—not every scholarship is so difficult to qualify for. There are so many opportunities, granting anywhere from a few hundred to several thousand dollars, that sometimes you'll get it just by virtue of being one of the only people who applied!

I always lean toward scholarships, because there's absolutely no requirement to repay anything. Grants are another similar option, and they're available on local, state, and federal levels. However, if free aid isn't an option for you, you'll have to look at loans.

There are plenty of options for loans and a ton of financial advice from people far better equipped than me to offer it, so take your time researching the matter, exercise caution, and consider talking to government institutions for more information. My best advice here is not in the matter of the loans themselves, but not to fear them so much that you miss an opportunity.

You may also consider studying abroad! College in Europe, for example, is *vastly* cheaper than college in the US, and in some cases is even free! Consider looking into overseas study programs in your area; some may even pay you to study abroad.

Going to college is an invaluable experience, and for a vast majority of people, debt is just part of the experience. It's not the end of the world! However long it takes, you *will* be able to pay it off, and live a good life in the meantime.

I managed to land a decent job, but I'm not in college and I'm still living with my parents. Everyone else my age seems like they have their stuff together already. Is it bad that I'm behind the curve? Does this make me a failure? *–Ann*

In the 21st century, we have to admit that it's not all that easy to get yourself up off the ground anymore.

The world today can be difficult to navigate, even for a two-income household. Whatever your reason for staying with your parents—finances, health, convenience, or even just preference—there is no shame in it. As well, there really isn't a time limit on higher education. As a matter of fact, there are programs all over the world to help even senior citizens start college courses and obtain degrees! It is never too late to start.

Besides, in many cultures, it's actually far more common for people to live with their parents until they are married, and sometimes even longer past that. It is good to live with a support system! So long as it doesn't put strain on the relationship you have with your parents, I think it's a good thing to continue cohabiting even after completing college.

We all have our own timelines in life, and whatever the case, you should listen to your own needs over the expectations of anyone else. Don't compare your success to another's.

So, to Recap:

- College is a path that branches into many different opportunities, so put a lot of careful consideration into your choices regarding education.

- If you don't want to go to college, there are countless other learning institutions or work prospects you can pursue.

- Even if school and work aren't options for you, there are still other avenues to pursue, so don't lose courage!

With all of this said and done, you should be well on your way to living a solid life and pursuing a good career. But you're only one girl, so next we'll address your best support throughout this journey: your family.

8

My Family Is My Ally

"Hi. I'm Bea, I'm 17, and... growing up is so much work. Friends and teachers come and go, and I don't know who I can trust to have my back through it all. I need support. How do I connect with my family, how can I make them understand, and how can I ask for their support?"

Growing up is such a wild and varied experience that it can feel really isolating. It's common for teen girls to feel that they're all alone in their experiences, and when told that your family is the best support in the world, it can be hard for you to believe it. After all, how can they understand what you're going through? What do they know about your experiences?

As it turns out, a *lot*. And even if they cannot personally relate, there is support to be found in family that you simply cannot find elsewhere. They are our built-in support systems, here for us when nobody and nothing else is. Don't waste this resource, and don't let your relationships with your family members waste away!

However, building and maintaining a relationship is a joint effort. As a show of trust, I will ask that both you and your guardian explore this chapter together.

You can take time to yourselves to read each section and consider or write your answers, or you can go over the chapter together and discuss the points as you go along. Use the questions that follow as talking points to have open, honest communication—and, above all, listen patiently to each other! You will each have time to say your piece.

For the Child

The very subject of this book, this first section focuses on you—the teen girl this guide was made for! Consider the following questions, and write down your answers if it helps you get your thoughts together.

Do You Feel Supported?

Starting a discussion with your family on the topic of support can be especially difficult if you do not already feel supported in any way.

Consider the things your family does for you already.

This can be as simple as taking care of your basic needs, or things that go the extra mile such as cheering you up or giving you gifts without being asked. What efforts do you notice your family putting forth? How much do you appreciate those efforts, and how do they make you feel?

Then, consider where your family does not support you. Are there any times that you feel brushed off or not cared for? What do they do, and how does it make you feel? Hurt, angry, or sad?

It is important to consider both the good and bad things they do. Compare them side by side, and ask yourself the question: Do you feel supported by them, overall? Whether you feel generally positively or negatively will help determine how much work you both need to put in.

How Can Your Family Improve?

Having noted where you feel your family is lacking, it's time to really dig into those issues.

It's easy to point at a singular instance and call it a fluke, or to only address that one behavior and nothing else. Afterward, some other conflict will pop up, and the conflict will start anew. What you need to do is get to the root of the problem, and have a conversation about *those* issues.

Ask yourself why certain things upset you. For example, if you are angry that your parents push too many chores on you, it could mean that you feel they don't value your time or take your exhaustion seriously. If you find yourself regularly arguing over your school performance, then it could be that you think they care more about grades than your well-being.

Often, lying underneath trivial arguments are deeper, more crucial problems that need to be clarified and addressed. Dive into the root of these conflicts, and try to express calmly why exactly these things upset you so much.

What would make you feel better, and what could help avoid future conflict? A change in the language used between you and your family? Easing up on certain responsibilities or expectations? Discuss together what you can do to make things easier for you both.

How Can You Help Your Family?

While there is undoubtedly plenty that your family can do for you, the reality is that there are always two sides to a conflict. You have a hand in the way things play out, and if you do not make any changes of your own, there is a very good chance that everything will go right back to how it was before.

133

The goal is not to seek revenge or to turn the tables, but to make everyone happier and healthier. Do not wish failure upon them, and be kind and gentle with any corrections or reminders. When you notice them putting forth effort, express your appreciation. The *most* valuable help you can provide your family is to show them patience. People do not change overnight; habits and learned behaviors can take a long time to adjust.

Your own attitude in the matter is the greatest factor under your control. If you punish good behavior with poor reactions, you are showing them that you will be unhappy no matter what, so there is no motivation for them to improve.

For the Adult

Now, it is time to turn things over to your parent or guardian.

Improving relations with your teen is a mutual effort. The fact that your child is bringing this section to your attention at all is a good sign! They are reaching out, and putting trust in you to try this out as a team. So, keep an open mind, and be patient with your child and with me as we walk through the following questions.

As has been encouraged with your child, consider writing down your answers to discuss afterward. This way you have plenty of time to ruminate on them, and you can avoid the responses being overly defensive or avoidant. The key objective of this chapter is to foster understanding!

Are You a Supportive Guardian?

Caretakers really do try their best. Navigating this world is hard enough when you only have yourself to worry about; throwing a dependent into the mix can absolutely throw things upside-down. So, first and foremost, I want you to know that I absolutely see and understand your struggles and that, even if your teen fails to fully understand the efforts you make, you should be proud of yourself for making it this far.

That being said, even in the best of parenting cases, perfection is still a long way off.

It is easy to fall into the common excuses that you are the adult, you have more experience, and you always know better. Unfortunately, the world is not that simple; even if you *are* more capable than a teenager, we, as adults, are not infallible. Should you overlook the true complications of the matter and the independence and care that your child needs beyond the basics, you will send yourself and your kid *both* down a path of mutual destruction. It is one thing to make sure your child's needs such as food, water, and shelter are met, and another to call yourself a truly supportive parent.

There are the more obvious questions when it comes to determining if your parent–child relationship has soured. Do you find yourself frequently arguing? Is your teen quick to talk back to you, or do you find that you just cannot keep your temper in check with them? Is there a lack of appreciation for one another's efforts? These are all quite clear indicators that something is wrong.

However, even if you are a generally nice parent, it can still be easy to fall absent and lack in other ways. How often do you and your child speak? Do you partake in any mutually enjoyable activities? Are you aware of any struggles your child is facing right now? How much do you actually know about your child's favorite things, friends, or out-of-school activities?

Think back on *recent* interactions when you ask yourself these things; time passes faster for us than it does for teenagers. Between work and bills, we can blink and an entire month is gone, whereas for your child that time has taken an eternity to pass. Arguments and incidents are more fresh in their mind than the nice outing you had 2 months ago.

If you find that your answer to the question of supportive parenting is an unsatisfactory one, don't worry! We're here to make it better. A healthy amount of guilt can incite change, but too much will just drag you down past a productive point. Patience with yourself is just as important in this matter as it is with your teenager.

How Can You Better Assist Your Teen?

As much as conflict is a mutual effort, when it comes to improving things, you have to understand that as an adult you are inevitably going to have to take more responsibility in this matter.

Teenagers are going through a time of unprecedented change and turmoil in their lives. Even reactions that seem like exaggerations to you are often genuine to them; as they've seen so little life, every bad thing that occurs could legitimately be the next worst event. They're quicker to turn to defensiveness, take longer to move on from unpleasant things, and can really hold grudges. While it is absolutely important to teach your child how to let go of conflict, it is equally important to understand that they will have a harder time with this than you and to be patient if they continue to lash out.

Patience and understanding are key. Look at unsavory behaviors and try to understand them, rather than seeing them as a reflection of your child's character; kids are rarely truly malicious. Your child could be hurting or angry for any number of reasons, and kids of any age can be absolutely terrible at articulating their feelings. If your child is trying to open up to you, do not interrupt them, do not correct them, and do not dismiss them.

Listen, acknowledge, discuss, and know when to apologize. It may take time, but as you build a more positive rapport, your teen will also be more willing to be patient with you.

How Can Your Teen Help You Improve?

Though much of the work will inevitably fall on your shoulders—having to be the mature one is rough work, for sure—there are things you can ask of your teen to make things easier.

Be honest and straightforward that this will require effort from you both, and that you're going to need patience from them. Be direct about why you may struggle; teenagers appreciate honesty, and breaking down that barrier of untouchability that parents sometimes have will encourage them to be more understanding toward you. Do not be afraid to ask your teen to elaborate on things or explain their feelings; making an effort to understand, however you might struggle, is something they will embrace.

It is okay to ask for your teen's consideration of your time. You're undoubtedly a very busy person, likely quite stressed, and you cannot attend to your child's every need. So long as you still make an effort to talk regularly, your child will be able to show patience and wait until you are ready.

Strengthen Your Bond

Here, we come to the question of what you can both do to improve your relationship. Fixing a negative thing is one issue, and enforcing positivity is another. It is absolutely a good thing to lack animosity in your relationship, but are you two close? If you aren't, what can you do to remedy that?

Plenty of things, really, from everyday habits to special activities! Read through the following list together, discuss your favorites, and plan together how you can incorporate these into your lives going forward.

Identify Your Love Languages

It's *unbelievably* easy to feel unappreciated and unwanted when in reality, you just don't have the same love language. If you don't express affection the same way, you can find yourself feeling neglected rather quickly. Discuss the following love languages, and determine which best suits you both.

- **Acts of service.** This is about taking the workload off of someone else, performing acts that take effort such as chores or errands so that the other person does not have to.

- **Gift-giving.** It is exactly how it sounds—you express affection by offering material goods to people you care about. Whether these are made or bought is irrelevant; they are a representation of your care for the other person.

- **Physical touch.** You appreciate physical contact with others, expressing love not only through kisses and hugs, but also by holding hands, linking arms, or even just offering high fives.

- **Quality time.** You want to spend time with other people that you can both enjoy, be it a mutual activity, engaging conversation, or just good old relaxation.

- **Words of encouragement.** You place a high value on complimenting others and expressing verbal or written approval and affirmations.

Try to pay attention to one another's love language, and take notice when you are expressing love toward one another that may otherwise go unnoticed. When things are especially rough or communications are failing, consider speaking one another's language. Give a gift where you usually wouldn't, or set time aside for a hug or cuddle. This can help really bridge the gap between you.

Do Things Together

This is easy to say, but not always so easy to do. It's not the most common for adults and children to have overlapping interests, after all. Teenage interests can come and go quickly or be hard to keep up with, while adults are often too busy, or their interests are outdated or less accessible.

Still, there are ways to overcome this! Consider the following activities.

Try to teach each other a favored skill or hobby.

With no pressure to succeed or necessary intentions to continue pursuing the skill, set time aside to teach each other something. It's easy for a parent to miss out on individuality in the midst of responsibilities, so the child can learn something new about their caretaker; as well, the teenager can have a chance to feel in control, and it is a good feeling to be the authority on something for once.

Find new things to try together. Be it learning a new skill, going to a new restaurant or store, watching a new show, or discovering local attractions worth exploring, finding something you are *both* unfamiliar with puts you on an even footing. This encourages you both to rely more on one another, rather than one of you taking charge. It can also create a mutual interest you would not have found otherwise.

Take turns planning outings. While it's good to take into consideration one another's preferences, you should also keep an open mind when it comes to potential shared activities. Having faith in one another to plan something enjoyable is a great way to increase trust and bond, and through this, you can gain a better understanding of what you each like. After you have a firm grasp on preferences, you can really make each other feel appreciated by planning around what the other person enjoys.

Allow Time and Space

As important as your bond is, you need to be mindful that you are not overdoing it. While familial bonds are easily the most crucial relationships to a teen's growth and development, it is also the case that they should not be *everything*. Just as friends cannot replace family, a family cannot replace friends. Children get the best social experience and development from their interactions with people outside of the family, as it is the best way to expose them to new ideas and encourage their individualism. Additionally, it is healthiest for adults to have friends their own age who they can confide in. Make sure that your relationship is not taking over the time that you *both* should be spending with friends.

As well, you don't want to overwhelm each other with your presence. People who live together, in particular, are especially prone to getting sick and tired of one another; if you find yourselves getting more snappy than usual, know that you may just need some time away from each other. Overexposure can lead to silly, petty fights that you would never have normally.

Finally, remember that conflict is not the end of your hard work. Even the best of friends are likely to fight. Take all the time you need to cool off, while not allowing problems to fester; do not force resolutions, but come together to discuss them when you are ready.

Q&A

No matter what I do, my parents just won't listen. They don't hear me out or even try to talk. I feel like they don't care. Who else can I turn to? —*Cass*

This is a really tough situation to be in.

As kids, our family is meant to be our greatest support, our first line of defense, our loudest cheerleaders. When that isn't the case, it can be extremely isolating. You might feel lonely or helpless, but you're still not alone.

A good place to start to find family support is your extended family. Aunts and uncles, grandparents, and even older cousins—these are all valid options. A trusted third party within the family can help bridge the gap between yourself and your guardians. If that fails, you've still found someone you can trust and confide in.

Even if there isn't someone within your family, there are adults all around you who you can confide in. Role models can be found at school, church, or even the families of your friends. What family you do not already have, you can build for yourself.

My mom and I have a good relationship, but I can tell she doesn't really know what she's doing when it gets to the hard stuff. She doesn't know what to say or do and sometimes I just come out of it feeling worse. If not my mom, then who is supposed to help me? –Rose

While our parents are much older and wiser than us, the unfortunate reality is that they don't know everything. As humans, we can only understand as much as we are exposed to, and within those parameters, we can still have a very shortsighted point of view. No matter how hard we try, there are times we just don't have the answer, and that's okay.

As much as we want to have all the answers, it's okay to look for help elsewhere. The best thing your guardians can do is have your back while you try other avenues. Ask them to help you find books on the topic, or even research it together with you. If it gets to the point you want to seek professional aid, they can still assist in finding the best resources for you and ensuring your needs are being met.

A good parent will know when it's best to let someone else take the wheel. Still, make sure to show them your utmost appreciation for the help they've already been, and assure them that you're thankful.

So, to Recap:

- The most valuable asset you have as a teenager is your family.

- Seek to build relationships and foster trust through mutual effort.

- Understand where you yourself factor into the equation of trust and understanding.

Growing up can be a scary experience all on your own. With your family on your side, there is nothing you cannot accomplish! Don't be afraid to lean on them for help.

Conclusion

Being a teenager is *difficult*.

I have already mentioned that when I was growing up, my mother really struggled to raise me in the way a teenage girl needed raising. Now that I'm older, I understand why she had such a hard time; after reading this book, I'm sure you can figure it out, too! As a teen girl, there are a hundred different worries you might experience, and oftentimes, you'll feel very alone in your journey. It is important to remember that no matter how difficult things get, you are not alone, and you will persevere!

Between teaching you about yourself, guiding you through social development, and preparing you for your future, this book has endeavored to teach you everything you need to survive your teenage years. From the very first buddings of physical maturity to the day you leave the nest, there is plenty of advice to move you past even the worst obstacles you may face.

This is only the beginning of your journey; every topic we've discussed so far could have books upon books written about them, and many of them do! Still, this is a powerful starting point, and it equips you with the tools you need. Even if you need more support further down the line, you have all of the knowledge at your fingertips on how you can make that happen.

And now? Now, you are ready to face the world as a strong young woman! Go out there with your head held high and your shoulders straight. Be true to yourself, remember the advice you've been given, and remember—you are not alone, so don't be afraid to lean on others for help!

References

Ahmed, E. (2022, October 5). *Use of social media by teens: Pros and cons.* Social Media Magazine. https://www.socialmediamagazine.org/use-of-social-media-by-teens-pros-cons/

Barrell, A. (2022, April 29). *At what age do girls stop growing?* Medical News Today. https://www.medicalnewstoday.com/articles/320668

BigFuture. (n.d.). *The types of colleges: The basics.* https://bigfuture.collegeboard.org/plan-for-college/college-basics/types-of-colleges/types-of-colleges-the-basics

The Bronfenbrenner Center for Translational Research. (2021, October 16). *The pros and cons of social media for youth.* Psychology Today. https://psychologytoday.com/us/blog/evidence-based-living/202110/the-pros-and-cons-social-media-youth

Bruce, D. F. (2020, November 12). *Teens and acne.* WebMD. https://www.webmd.com/skin-problems-and-treatments/acne/what-is-acne

Buel, Z. (2019, September 3). *What is a trade job?* Tulsa Welding School & Technology Center. https://www.tws.edu/blog/skilled-trades/what-is-a-trade-job/

Cleveland Clinic. (2022a, March 15). *Pimple popping 101: How to (safely) zap your zits.* https://health.clevelandclinic.org/pimple-popping-101-how-to-safely-zap-your-zits/

Cleveland Clinic. (2022b, August 12). *Toxic shock syndrome (TSS).* https://my.clevelandclinic.org/health/diseases/15437-toxic-shock-syndrome

Creative Faze. (2017, July 25). *Website development and why people use internet.* https://www.creativefaze.com/website-development-and-why-people-use-internet

Doyle, A. (2021, August 19). *How to get your first part-time job for teens.* The Balance. https://www.thebalancemoney.com/tips-for-getting-your-first-part-time-job-2058650

Ehmke, R. (2023, February 22). *Teens and romantic relationships.* Child Mind Institute.

https://childmind.org/article/how-to-help-kids-have-good-romantic-relationships/

Grabinski, A. (2023, April 6). *How to find your personal style, once and for all.* The Everygirl. https://theeverygirl.com/tips-find-personal-style/

Grossman, A. L. (2022, May 18). *How to get a job as a teenager (your teen's 3-week plan).* Money Prodigy. https://www.moneyprodigy.com/how-to-get-a-job-as-a-teenager/

Hackett, F. (2023, February 6). *Tips for teens: How to find your first real job.* Resume Builder. https://www.resumebuilder.com/tips-for-teens-how-to-find-your-first-real-job/

Hatcher, J. P. (2017, December 6). *20 pros and cons of social media use.* SUCCESS. https://www.success.com/20-pros-and-cons-of-social-media-use/

HealthDirect Australia. (2023, April 28). *Puberty for girls*. https://www.healthdirect.gov.au/puberty-for-girls

Healthwise Staff. (2021, November 17). *Learning about safer sex for teens*. My Health Alberta. https://myhealth.alberta.ca/health/AfterCareInformation/pages/conditions.aspx?hwid=av2956

Hudson, A. (2022, October 19). *13 ways on how to help your teen make friends*. Ashley Hudson Therapy. https://www.ashleyhudsontherapy.com/post/13-ways-on-how-to-help-your-teen-make-friends

Intercoast Colleges. (2021, August 4). *6 factors to consider when choosing trade schools*. https://intercoast.edu/blog/choosing-trade-schools/

IPSY. (n.d.). *Calling all makeup beginners! This expert-approved makeup guide is for you.*

https://www.ipsy.com/blog/makeup-for-beginners

John Hopkins All Children's Hospital. (2020, November 16). *What is a growth spurt during puberty?* https://www.hopkinsallchildrens.org/ACH-News/General-News/What-is-a-Growth-Spurt-During-Puberty

John Miur Health. (n.d). *Nutrition for teens.* https://www.johnmuirhealth.com/health-education/health-wellness/childrens-health/nutrition-teens.html

Mahan, B. (2022, April 30). *How to heal a strained parent-teenager relationship.* ADDitude. https://www.additudemag.com/parent-teenager-relationship-building-strategies/

Manjunatha, F. (2021, January 20). *13 tips for managing teen acne.* Mayo Clinic Health System. https://www.mayoclinichealthsystem.org/homet

own-health/speaking-of-health/tips-for-managing-teen-acne

Matthews, V., & Cheema, S. (2023, May 25). *45 summer jobs for teens with better pay than ever.* The Penny Hoarder. https://www.thepennyhoarder.com/make-money/summer-jobs-for-teens/

McCracken, K. (2021, May 7). *Period products: What teens need to know.* Nationwide Children's. https://www.nationwidechildrens.org/family-resources-education/700childrens/2021/05/period-products-teens

Michaels, C. (2023). *Taking care of yourself under stress.* University of Minnesota Extension. https://extension.umn.edu/taking-care-yourself-under-stress

North Carolina Department of Information Technology. (n.d.). *Online safety tips for teens.* https://it.nc.gov/resources/online-safety-privacy/tips-guidance/online-safety-tips-teens

Noble, A. (2021, May 10). *Four expert-approved tips for finding your signature everyday makeup look.* Martha Stewart. https://www.marthastewart.com/8098922/how-create-signature-makeup-look

Paradigm Treatment. (2017, May 1). *Why teens need opportunities for self-discovery.* https://paradigmtreatment.com/teens-opportunities-self-discovery/

pH-D Feminine Health. (2022, November 23). *Vaginal care & feminine hygiene tips for teenage girls.* https://www.phdfemininehealth.com/blogs/articles/feminine-hygiene-tips-for-teenage-girls

PsychAlive. (2015, August 28). *A guide to finding yourself.* https://www.psychalive.org/finding-yourself/

Raising Children Network (Australia). (2021, April 23). *Hygiene: pre-teens and teenagers.* https://raisingchildren.net.au/pre-teens/healthy-lifestyle/hygiene-dental-care/hygiene-pre-teens-teens

ReachOut. (n.d.-a). *Self-care and teenagers.* https://parents.au.reachout.com/skills-to-build/wellbeing/self-care-and-teenagers

ReachOut. (n.d.-b). *Teenagers making friends – can parents help?* https://parents.au.reachout.com/skills-to-build/wellbeing/things-to-try-friendships/teenagers-making-friends-can-parents-help

The Royal Women's Hospital. (n.d.). *Food and nutrition for adolescents.* https://www.thewomens.org.au/health-information/staying-well/adolescent-girls/food-and-nutrition-for-adolescents

Scott, E. (2023, April 17). *What is spirituality?* Verywell Mind. https://www.verywellmind.com/how-spirituality-can-benefit-mental-and-physical-health-3144807

Stanford Medicine Children's Health. (n.d.). *Exercise and teenagers.* https://www.stanfordchildrens.org/en/topic/default?id=exercise-and-teenagers-90-P01602

Tan, R. (2020, December 7). *7 things you can do to improve your relationship with your parents.* SmileTutor. https://smiletutor.sg/7-things-you-can-do-to-improve-your-relationship-with-your-parents/

Together Teens&20s. (n.d). *What Should I Do After High School?* St. Jude Children's Research Hospital. https://together.stjude.org/en-us/teensand20s/adulting-with-cancer/life-after-high-school.html

U.S. Army. (2021, September 10). *Take charge of your present and future.* https://www.goarmy.com/benefits.html

University of the People. (2023, February 17). *What to do after high school? Get a plan!* https://www.uopeople.edu/blog/things-i-wish-i-knew-when-i-graduated-high-school/

U.S. Government. (n.d.). *Military pay and benefits.* https://www.usa.gov/military-pay-benefits

Wake Counseling & Mediation. (2017, May 5). *Apply these 6 techniques to improve parent-teen relationship.*

https://www.wakecounseling.com/therapy-blog/improve-parent-teen-relationship

WebMD Editorial Contributors. (2022, December 7). *Shaving tips for teen girls.* WebMD. https://teens.webmd.com/shaving-tips-girls

WebMD Editorial Contributors. (2023, May 29). *Difference between deodorant and antiperspirant.* WebMD. https://www.webmd.com/skin-problems-and-treatments/difference-between-deodorant-and-antiperspirant

Zinn, D. (2020, September 23). *How to pay for college: 5 ways to fund your education now.* Forbes Advisor. https://www.forbes.com/advisor/student-loans/how-to-pay-for-college/